If you're a lawyer who's had little or no training in how to attract your ideal clients, and you're suspicious of traditional marketing and sales tactics, then this book is for you.

In it, I'll show you how to attract and convert the quantity – and quality – of clients you want, without ever compromising your integrity or feeling uncomfortable.

From my own experience as a practising lawyer, I understand why many lawyers are reluctant to take any action that might feel unprofessional. But I promise there's a sweet spot between the kind of marketing which is overly 'salesy', and that which plays it so safe that it produces no results at all.

This book will share my key strategies for success and the results that following them has brought to others like you. Along the way, I'll prove that you don't have to choose between being professional and being successful at selling your services. By reading this book and following the steps I recommend, you can be both.

THE
CLIENT MAGNET
FORMULA
— FOR LAWYERS —

THE
CLIENT MAGNET
FORMULA
—— FOR LAWYERS ——

How to **attract** and **convert**
more of your ideal clients

MICHELLE PETERS

SOLICITOR (NON-PRACTISING)

The Client Magnet Formula for Lawyers

First published 2019

This book is not intended to provide personalised legal, financial or professional ethics advice. Before starting any new marketing or business development initiatives you should always check with your local law society or bar standards board that you meet your professional standards requirements. The author specifically disclaims any liability, loss or risk which is incurred as a consequence (directly or indirectly) of the use and application of any of the content of this book.

Author: Michelle Peters
Cover design: Katie Bell
Cover image: Alphaspirit/Shutterstock.com
ISBN 978-1-7986-3412-7

CONTENTS

PREPARE

Chapter 1
Getting Started

What is the Client Magnet Formula?

The Client Magnet Formula enables you to dramatically increase the number of ideal clients you bring into your practice, allowing you the freedom to work only with clients who appreciate you and don't quibble about your fees.

The Formula consists of my Client Attraction and Client Conversion Systems, which are combined to enable you to identify who your ideal clients are, and then *attract* more enquiries from them and *convert* more of them into paying clients.

It will allow you to do so without having to *sell* your services. Instead, it will attract enquiries from your ideal clients, and persuade them to say "yes" to instructing you at the fees you want to charge, by showing them the 'four whys': *why* they need your service; *why* they should obtain your help sooner rather than later; *why* it's worth investing in your services; and *why* they should specifically choose you.

How to use this book

Here are my recommendations:

1. Don't skip the fundamentals (the *9 Key Principles* to attracting and converting more of your ideal clients). Without them it'll be like trying to build a house without foundations.

2. Start with either 'Attract' or 'Convert', depending on which you consider you most need.

3. Look out for helpful signposts:

   a. Takeaways – bite-sized summaries of the content

   b. Success Tips – advanced moves to accelerate your results

   c. Action Steps – your homework (nothing will change unless you take action).

4. Use the resources and checklists at www. clientmagnetformula.com (make sure to register for updates and notifications of new tools as they become available).

Note: In this book I use the term 'marketing' to refer to any action used to attract new clients. This means it covers a wide array of business development activities such as networking, writing articles, running seminars or talks, websites, adverts in newspapers, online advertising, and 'pay-per-click' marketing.

Before you start: do you have the right mindset to grow your practice?

In the next chapter we'll look in detail at why it might not be your fault that you don't yet have the clients and income you deserve.

But first, I'd like you to consider whether there's something else that might be holding you back and sabotaging your success: too much *knowing* and not enough *doing*.

"To know and not to do is really not to know", said Dr Stephen R Covey in his book 'The 7 Habits of Highly Effective People'.

In other words, knowledge without action doesn't change things. *Action* changes things.

So, as you read this book, listen out to that little voice in your head. If it's saying, *"I already know this"* then I want you to ask yourself, *"Yes, but am I **doing** it?"*

If you are, then give yourself a brief pat on the back before asking, *"But can I improve the **way** I'm doing it?"* If the answer is "no", then that's great news (as long as it's really true!). If, however, the answer is "yes", then your mission is to find out how you could improve it – whether with the help of this book, or with more direct support from an expert (perhaps me).

And if you're thinking *"I've tried that but it doesn't work"*, remember that failure is only a signal that you haven't yet found the right way to do something. Perhaps it's also a signal that, just like your clients, you might need the support of an expert before you get it right.

3

Chapter 2
What's Stopping You From Having The Clients You Want?

If you're reading this, I'm going to assume you don't have as many of your *ideal* clients as you really want. And I'll also bet this has nothing to do with your skills as a lawyer.

In which case, you're not alone.

You've probably spent thousands of hours honing your legal skills, both in training and in practice.

Maybe you're a general practitioner who advises clients on many different areas of law, so you need to spend a lot of time keeping up with developments in all the areas in which you practise.

Or maybe you're a specialist in, for example, corporate law, employment, or intellectual property, and you need to spend time making sure you know everything there is to know about legal and practice developments in your specific area.

Either way, I'm sure you get great results for your existing clients and they gladly refer you when they can.

If, however, you're like the majority of lawyers I speak to who don't have as many clients as they want – or at least not enough of the *right type* – being an excellent lawyer doesn't necessarily translate into being a successful one.

So what's going on?

The skills gap

The short answer is that being good at the *practise* of law is not the same as being good at the *business* of law. And law *is* a business, just like any other.

The most successful lawyers (the ones with all the clients and the profits to match) are invariably good at the business *and* the practise of law.

They're good at attracting the right kinds of clients; good at converting new enquiries into loyal clients; good at collecting fees and managing expectations; good at keeping clients happy – not just by providing good legal services but by providing a good client experience. And, finally, they're good at maximising their profits from each client whilst remaining ethical and professional.

How many times have you looked at a competitor and thought, *"I'm just as good a lawyer as them and yet they seem to get all the clients (and profits)"*? I hear this all the time. The chances are they're simply better at getting clients than you are.

So what's stopping you from being that kind of lawyer?

Maybe you haven't – yet – devoted the time and effort you need to learn the skills to attract the right kinds of clients – those who will keep your practice full and profitable. Or maybe you haven't – yet – focused on how best to service your clients so they instruct you more often, and refer you more frequently to others.

Commonly, when I ask attendees at the seminars I run what percentage of their learning and development time they spend on legal training compared to business skill development training, their answers mostly hover around the 70:30 to 90:10 mark. (Some even admit to spending no time at all on developing their business skills.)

So, if I were to ask you the same question, what would you answer?

If it's less than 30%, then it shouldn't be any surprise that your business skills aren't as advanced as your legal skills. Nor should it be a surprise that you don't have as many ideal clients as you'd like.

If you want to be more successful, you must first accept that you need to improve your skills in attracting and converting enquiries from the right kinds of prospective clients.

How skills impact profits

These skills are not only vital to achieving results, they're also vital to ensuring you get the clients you want *quickly* and *efficiently*. As we all know, law is generally a 'time for money' model, which means that every hour you spend away from fee-earning is an hour of billable time (and profit) lost. This is why it's so vital to leverage (that is, make the most of) your time by spending as little of it as possible in attracting each client, and as much of it as possible in providing billable services to these clients.

To give an example, let's say that your legal practice currently attracts ten new clients a month. To generate each new enquiry you need to have spent time on marketing, networking, writing articles, or on some other business development activity. You then need to spend time talking to each prospective client to see how you can help them and, if they decide to proceed, to talk them through the necessary next steps. However, not every enquiry will turn into a new client, so some of this time will end up being wasted.

If we take an example where, on average, it takes five hours to complete both steps for each client, then – at ten new clients – it means you'd be spending 50 hours a month on this. The cost to you of this time is equivalent to the hourly rate you'd be charging if you were fee-earning. At a (modest) rate of £200 an hour, the cost to your practice would be £10,000 (50 x £200). In other words, the cost of gaining those ten new clients significantly reduces the overall profits they generate. So if, for example, the average value of each new client is £2,000 but they cost £1,000 to acquire, then your gross profit will be only £1,000 – and that's before you take into account overheads and salaries.

So you might well be making considerably less profit per client than you realise.

If, however, you could spend *half* the amount of time getting each new client then one of two things would happen:

1. **you would free up** 25 hours to work on client matters which would allow you to generate £5,000 (25 x £200) extra revenue a month; or

2. **you could double** the number of new clients you acquire from the 50 hours you spend, which would reduce the cost of gaining each one by half, and therefore increase the gross profit each generates by 50%. Continuing the above example, you

would now have 20 new clients paying £2,000 each with gross profit of £1,500 from each client.

This is why it's so important for you to develop the **right** skills to attract and convert the **right** new clients – it has a direct effect on profitability.

Why it's not your fault you don't yet have the skills you need

If you're feeling uncomfortable about the fact that you're lacking in key skills to grow your practice, then I have some good news.

It's not your fault.

It's not your fault because most professional firms simply don't teach client-attraction and client-conversion skills – however essential these may be. They certainly didn't teach me at the firm where I worked. Instead, training is often focused on the 'hard' legal skills with, at the most, a brief nod to 'soft' skills such as communication, teamwork, and negotiation. Indeed, client attraction (marketing) and conversion (sales) is generally not offered as part of a lawyer's professional development. Even when it is, it's often out of date or not tailored to the specific needs of each lawyer and their clients.

It's also not your fault because you're probably simply following in the footsteps of the senior lawyers who taught you your craft. But – for reasons we'll explore in the next chapter – times have changed, and what worked for them then won't necessarily work for you now.

Similarly, it's not your fault if you think that because you get good results from your current networking activities or a reasonable number of referrals from clients and other professionals, you've already got marketing covered. Whilst – due to the lack of spare time that virtually all lawyers suffer from – there may not be any more hours you can physically devote to networking or to meeting new professionals, there's certainly a lot more you can do to make networking and referrals more effective. As you'll soon discover from this book, one of these is to add the Client Magnet Formula to your networking activities and to use it with your referrers.

What's more, networking and referrals are *inherently limited* ways of growing your practice. It requires time to travel to, attend, and follow up on networking events. This means that, because your time is finite, networking simply isn't scaleable. Referrals are similarly limited by the opportunity (or whim) of your contacts.

If you really want to grow your practice, and to be in control of both the speed and the size of the growth, then you need to put in place scaleable marketing and growth strategies that are within your direct control. In other words, strategies you can activate whenever *you* want (without waiting for others to act) and which enable you to get bigger or faster results without investing more time. These strategies require a new approach and new skills to implement them.

This is what the Client Magnet Formula provides.

Can you really remain professional and develop the skills you need to 'sell' your services?

If you'd asked me this question 15 years ago I might have said "No".

At that time I was a lawyer in private practice at a large international firm. Like most lawyers I know, I didn't receive any training on how to win clients. And even though I'd worked there for nine years, I had virtually no experience of marketing – beyond the occasional pitch presentation for existing clients, writing a few articles for law journals, and networking events where I invariably ended up talking to people I already knew. (Even more embarrassingly, they were usually people from my own firm.) I really had no experience of selling my services at all – I just did the work I was given by existing clients or by partners in the firm.

Not only did I have very little experience of marketing or selling, but I'd have run a mile if you'd asked me to do either. I simply didn't consider them to be things that a professional should have to do. Surely just being good at what I did was enough?

It wasn't until I left private practice that I learned the hard way that being good at what you do does not guarantee you clients. No matter how hard you're prepared to work, without clients you don't have a business.

I left private practice at the end of 2004 (because I wanted to take a sabbatical to go skiing for 3 months and resigning was the only way to make it possible – it's a long story). To give me a focus whilst I was figuring out what I wanted to do next I offered to help my father with franchising his business. Although I only planned to be there on a short-term basis (to set up the legal framework for franchising), before I knew it I'd been there for five years! During that time I became the Director of Franchising with responsibility for recruiting, training, and mentoring our franchisees.

My new role included helping franchisees with their marketing. I'd always been interested in advertising and marketing, and I'd briefly flirted with the idea of going into advertising before deciding to become a lawyer.

I learned a lot from my father, who taught me the key marketing and selling principles he'd learned over the years (including from marketing guru Drayton Bird, with whom he'd worked). I soon discovered that marketing was difficult, unpredictable, frustrating, and costly. But the thrill of seeing the results when I got it right was enough to keep me coming back.

I was hooked and wanted to know more. I took some courses and started to explore the mix of creative and scientific elements that go into successfully persuading clients or customers to buy what you have to offer.

Fast forward five years and I'd learned so much about not only marketing and sales, but also key business skills like strategic planning, cashflow forecasting, and analysing profitability. I was in a whole new world.

When my father and I decided to exit the business in 2010, I once again found myself wondering what to do next. I briefly considered going back into private practice, but I realised – somewhat to my surprise – how much more I'd enjoyed growing a business (and helping our franchisees to do the same) than I had enjoyed my time as a lawyer.

That's why I found myself drawn to the idea of helping lawyers and other professionals to grow their practice by developing the same business skills that I'd learned.

To give me credibility – and confidence – I decided to re-train in business development, marketing, and sales, investing £15,000 on a high-level course to become a certified business growth consultant and coach. Then, fresh from my training, I got my business cards printed and was ready to go.

However, here's where the irony comes in: when I first started my new role I struggled to get clients for myself.

How embarrassing is that? I was now supposed to be the expert in getting clients and growing a business, but I found that all the marketing and sales techniques I'd been taught didn't feel right when it came to promoting my own services to prospective clients. In fact, I found many of the techniques to be uncomfortable, unwelcome, and ultimately unworkable.

As a result, I couldn't bring myself to use them, which meant I didn't have a system to follow.

Conversion was a particular challenge. Although I was able to use some of the techniques I'd been taught to obtain meetings with prospective clients (such as offering to show them how to grow their business in a free meeting), I soon discovered that - despite dragging my heavy case full of marketing materials from meeting to meeting - providing free advice only led to resistance to paying for future advice. I also realised my positioning was all wrong because my marketing materials failed to show clients *why they needed me.*

Although many months brought no new clients at all, looking back this was probably a blessing: I was spending so much time looking for clients that I had very little left to actually do any work for them!

In my first year I worked really hard but had little to show for it other than a rapidly declining bank balance. It was then I realised that, if I was going to be successful, I'd need to forget the conventional teaching and find another way to attract and convert clients; one that would fit with both my professional approach and personality.

Finding this other way involved spending a lot of time and money on courses and training, followed by a period of considerable trial and error as I pieced together the parts that worked and felt right for me.

By the end of my second year I'd created my own Client Magnet Formula, which allowed me to do two things:

1. **Attract**: obtain enquiries from my ideal clients on a consistent and regular basis (persuading them to contact me rather than me chasing them).

2. **Convert**: turn enquiries into paying clients in a way which felt comfortable and ethical, and which helped clients see the value of my services (without the need to spend hours persuading them or giving my expertise away for free).

In the next 12 months I acquired many new clients and tripled my fee income – all without doing anything that felt unprofessional or 'salesy'.

Having used this Formula to attract and convert clients for myself with such success, I was ready to start teaching it to others. And, as confirmation that I was on the right track, I was delighted when it led to one of my first clients (a commercial lawyer) being able to increase enquiries by 30% over a six month period, with 36% more of these converted into new clients.

If you'd like to see similar results in your practice, this book will take you through the steps you need to take.

Chapter 3
Why You Need A New Approach

If you've been in practice for a while – or even if you've only recently started – you've probably noticed that it's getting harder and harder to attract and convert the right kinds of clients.

It's a complaint I hear all the time from lawyers who are looking for ways to improve the quality and quantity of their clients.

I'm not surprised – right now, we're in the middle of a perfect storm. And that storm is making it harder than ever to get clients.

The Perfect Storm

This storm is caused by three factors:

- advancements in technology;

- changes in the legal marketplace; and

- the traditional approach of law firms to attracting clients.

Although together these can form a barrier which may seem impenetrable, it isn't – as I'll soon show. But first, let's examine how these factors are getting in the way.

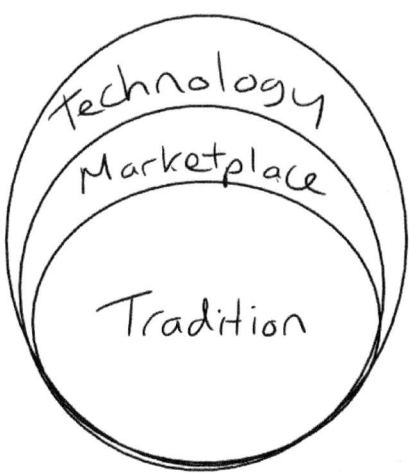

Technology: Developments in technology have brought many blessings for lawyers, from remote working to wider geographic markets and increased efficiencies. But some of these same developments can make it harder than ever to attract clients.

- **The end of local bias**: Clients no longer need to choose a lawyer whose offices are near to where they live or work. Now they can use lawyers based anywhere, by meeting with them online and sending documents electronically.

- **Comparison is easier**: Potential clients can shop around simply by comparing options (and prices) online.

- **The rise of DIY**: The ease with which legal information can be found online has not only led to a rise in DIY (particularly in areas such as family law and probate) but also to a lowering of the value of information in the minds of clients.

Legal marketplace: The marketplace is expanding rapidly. With the rise of alternative business structures and continuing moves to de-regulate parts of the legal services market, there are more and more competitors.

This expansion, combined with the ease with which potential clients can now shop around, means:

- increased competition;

- downward pressure on fees; and

- increasing difficulty in attracting the attention of potential clients.

The Traditional Approach of Law Firms: Many firms continue to use the "build it and they will come" approach, assuming that if they set up a firm clients will simply appear. In the past, this method probably brought them a fair share of the work that was available (in other words, a similar amount to their competitors), and that was enough to keep everyone's practice busy.

Now, though, the changes I've discussed above have resulted in less work and more providers, meaning a fair share is often not enough. In addition, whilst referrals and recommendations are great, you have no control over them. So you can't just decide one day that you want more referrals and expect them to land in your lap. That's why to be successful today you need an active client acquisition strategy; one where *you* control the results.

Even though many firms have realised this and have started to focus more on marketing and other business development activities, many quickly run into three major challenges:

1. **The marketing doesn't work**. There are many reasons why this happens, but two of the biggest are:

    -   A reluctance to appear to be selling services - for fear it may appear unprofessional - has held many lawyers back from anything other than very conservative marketing. (And because this frequently looks almost exactly the same as that of every other law firm, it's impossible to stand out.)

    -   A focus on *where* you do your marketing (the method) rather than *what your marketing contains* (the message). This prevents you from getting the right message to the right potential clients.

2. **Poor conversion rate**. Concentrating on attracting more enquiries without making sure that you have a good conversion rate (turning enquiries into paying clients) means that a large proportion of the time and money you spend on obtaining enquiries could be wasted.

3. **Inefficient use of fee-earner time**. Not devoting enough time and resources to improving the skills of staff (particularly fee-earners) – so that they're able to attract and convert client enquiries – results in wasted time. Either it takes too long to attract and convert a new client, or the time spent bears no fruit at all. Either way, client numbers and profits are reduced.

Overcoming the obstacles to win more clients

To overcome these challenges, three critical shifts are needed.

1. **Make sure your marketing stands out from your competitors *and* that it contains the right message to attract your ideal clients**

To do this, you need to change the content of your marketing to help prospective clients know *why* they need your help and *why* they should choose you. This one simple change will be enough to set you streets ahead of your competitors.

Telling them *why* starts with explaining the benefits they'll gain from using your services.

Many law firms concentrate on telling clients about the features of their product or services, listing these before going on to detail the amount of time they'll spend or the documents they'll produce. They then expect clients to work out the benefits for themselves.

This is *not* the best way to promote your services. Not only do clients frequently fail to translate *features* into *benefits*, but your marketing looks just like that of your competitors. If you follow the Client Magnet Formula your marketing will clearly explain the benefits of working with you, and you'll stand out.

Once a prospective client is convinced of the benefits of your service, their next question will be *"Are you the right person to provide it?"*

If you fail to explain *why* a prospective client should choose you (rather than one of your competitors), the chances are that many of them won't.

Let's face it, if you don't know the answer to this question – or simply forget to mention it – why should they put their trust in you in the first place?

However, I know from experience that many lawyers struggle with this. One of my employment lawyer clients could only think of one reason clients should choose her over competitors and, as she sheepishly told me it, it was clear she didn't feel it was strong enough to even mention. And she was right. It didn't differentiate her at all. But, by the end of our Client Magnet planning session, we had uncovered five compelling reasons why prospective clients *should* choose her – simply by putting ourselves in the shoes of her ideal client.

> **Takeaway:** *Always answer the fundamental question of every prospective client: "Why do I need your help and why should I choose you?"*
>
> *In Chapter 4 I'll go into more detail about how the Client Magnet Formula can help you answer this question, ensuring that prospective clients will give you the answer you want – a "yes" to working with you.*

2. Understand that gaining clients is about attracting more enquiries *and* converting these into paying clients

Many of the law firms I work with are already spending a lot of time and money on marketing. But attracting more enquiries is only one element of winning clients. The other – equally important – element is being able to convert those enquiries into paying clients at the minimum cost.

It costs time and money to attract new enquiries, so how successful you are at converting enquiries into paying clients will have a direct impact on your profitability.

If, for example, your current success rate is 1 in 3 but you increase that to 2 in 3, your number of new clients will double without any additional marketing or time spent on meeting prospective clients.

What would that mean for your practice?

Takeaway: *The easiest way to gain clients and to improve profitability – assuming you already have enquiries coming into your practice – is to focus on improving your conversion rate.*

A word of warning here: although many firms proudly tell me that their conversion rate is very high, a measurement of (say) 90% is often not the real picture because:

- They only include the success rate of converting an enquiry into a paying client after a meeting or phone consultation with a fee-earner – ignoring the significant percentage of enquiries which never get this far.

- They may be lowering their fees to get a "yes". (Reduced fees may lead to being busier but they result in less profit – and who really wants that?)

- This rate might be calculated on enquiries from referrals or former clients, who are the easiest to convert. To really grow you need to attract and convert cold enquiries – which requires a higher level of skill.

So always be clear about what your true conversion rate is in terms of turning enquiries from a variety of sources into paying clients at the fees you want to charge.

3. **Be clear about your area of expertise – where it is, and where it isn't**

As a lawyer, you probably have a specific area of expertise; or maybe you have several. But are you a specialist in *all* areas of law – from matrimonial to commercial property? Or from business sales to employment tribunal cases?

In my case, I specialised in intellectual property for seven years. I didn't have the same level of knowledge in other areas, like employment or corporate, because I hadn't had the same level of training or experience.

So why do some lawyers feel they should be expert in practice growth strategies and skills – particularly without any training or help?

If you want to attract more clients and grow your practice, then it's important to accept that you'll probably need help to improve your skills in areas such as attracting enquiries and converting more of these into paying clients.

The good news is that you're already an expert in one critical area: that of understanding what prospective clients need to know in order to choose your services. This means that you also know – even if you don't realise it yet – what they need to see or hear in your marketing, and in your initial conversations with them.

So now let's combine your expertise with mine to map out a client attraction and conversion strategy that will fill your practice – with the *right kinds* of clients – fast.

Do I really need to learn all these strategies and skills – can't I just delegate?

One of the most important lessons any practice owner needs to learn is how to market their business – because without clients you won't have one for long. Many people assume marketing is simply about deciding whether or not to do Facebook, or choosing where to run adverts and which networking events to attend. But, as I've explained, marketing is really about getting the *right message in front of the right audience* so that they enquire about your services.

And whilst attracting high quality enquiries is important, it's ultimately fruitless unless you turn those enquiries into paying clients. For most practice owners, this means learning how to 'sell' their services.

Of course, running a business isn't just about being able to bring in new work. You'll also need to create the right business model (one that's profitable and can be adapted as you grow), learn about finance (including cashflow, profit and loss and balance sheets) and be able to manage your staff so they can deliver a great service to your clients.

Yes, you can get help with all of these. But if you decide to outsource or delegate parts of your business you don't understand, you're heading for disaster. I can't tell you how many lawyers I've spoken to who've said, *"We tried advertising but it didn't work."* When, however, I push for more details by asking how they decided on the content of their adverts, they respond by saying that the advertising department of the newspaper or magazine put it together. In other words, not only did they not have a strategy for their advert, they didn't even play any part in deciding its content. Instead, they left it to someone who probably knew little – if anything – about their business. No wonder they had zero results!

This doesn't mean you need to get involved in every detail of your business – far from it. But it does mean you need to develop your business skills to a level that allows you to participate in setting the strategy for every part of your practice. That way, if you do decide to delegate the implementation of the strategy, you'll know whether or not it's being done correctly.

> **Takeaway:** Outsourcing or delegating your marketing without understanding the strategy that underpins it is like asking someone to build you a house without allowing you to have any input into its design, purpose, or cost. What are the chances you'll get the house you really want?

ATTRACT

Chapter 4
Client Attraction:
9 Key Principles

The 9 key principles of client attraction are like the foundations of a house. If you're tempted to skip the effort required to work on these principles, just remember that without them your marketing will be ineffective at best and, at worst, it'll be counter-productive – bringing you the kind of enquiries that take up your time without turning into instructions.

In other words, these principles directly affect not only the quality and quantity of enquiries you'll receive, but also your client conversion success rate. Skip them and you'll find it harder (and more costly) to obtain new clients, and less likely that you'll have the ideal clients you deserve.

Ready?

Principle 1: Know who you want to attract

I'm sure you've heard the saying *"You can't be all things to all people"*. And it's certainly true when it comes to attracting clients.

If you try to create marketing that will attract everyone you could possibly help, it's unlikely you'll get many enquiries. It won't be clear that you're talking to your ideal clients because your marketing will be too generic to catch their attention.

Not that this means you *can't* market to all of them. It just means that you need to create different – and specific – marketing for each type of client you want to attract.

For example, Andrew – a commercial lawyer – was struggling to attract the right kinds of clients when I met him. He was using what I call 'here I am' marketing – in other words, marketing which gave the name of his firm, the areas in which he practised (distribution agreements, business acquisitions and sales, and shareholder disputes) and explained how to contact him (email, address, phone number). He believed that by targeting business owners he was being specific. But business owners who want to sell their business aren't the same as those who want to buy one, just as those who need a distribution agreement aren't the same as those involved in a shareholder dispute.

That's why you need to pick just *one* type of client with *one* type of problem or need, and then create marketing *specifically* for *them*. Once you do this, you'll be able to use the Client Magnet Formula to its full potential.

Remember, this doesn't limit the type or number of clients you can attract. It's simply a case of choosing one type first, and then creating and using marketing specific to them. You can repeat the process for as many types as you like.

Action Steps:

1. Pick one specific client type that you want to attract for one specific service, and commit to creating marketing in the next 90 days that will attract them.

2. Make sure you choose a type of client or service that's both profitable and that you like. You can use the worksheet 'Identify Your Ideal Client' to help – download your copy at www.clientmagnetformula.com

---

Principle 2: If you don't want to sell, your marketing needs to help clients understand why they should buy

Most lawyers don't want to sell. They just want clients to appear, instruct them, and pay their bills without quibbling. I remember wanting that too.

But if you don't have enough clients (or simply enough of the *right* clients), then you already have all the evidence you need that this approach isn't working and that it's time to try something different.

If you're uncomfortable with 'selling' in your marketing (or the subsequent conversations with prospective clients), then you need to focus on persuading your prospective clients to *buy*.

And to persuade clients to buy you need to help them see that they *want* or *need* what you have to offer.

Buying things we *want* is fun. We enjoy buying a new watch or a new pair of shoes. Yes, we might be doing so because whatever we had before has broken, but often we buy things simply for the pleasure a new or better one brings.

We also buy less exciting things such as insurance, physiotherapy or legal advice. Few of us get delight from buying these, but we do so when we see that we *need* them. For example, we might see we need physiotherapy to get back on track after an injury, or decide we need legal advice if we're thinking of buying a company.

In other words, the reason we buy such services is that we *perceive* a need for them. We think we'll benefit in some way - that they'll solve a problem for us or help us to achieve a goal.

If, however, we don't think we need them *enough*, or that they'll cost us more than the benefit we'll receive, we won't buy them. We only buy when we *perceive* the cost to be less than the *benefit*.

Benefits must outweigh costs

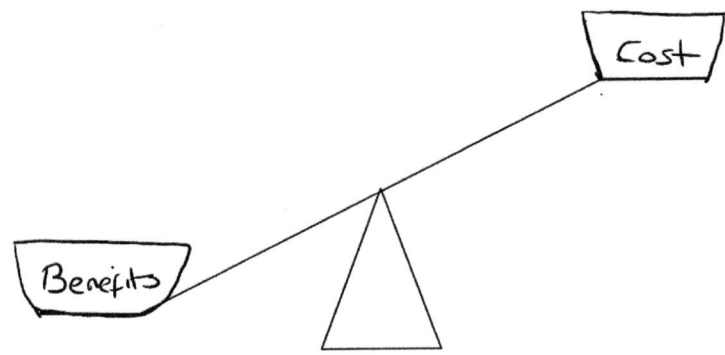

What influences our decision to buy?

There are things that motivate us to buy and things that demotivate us. Our motivators might include want, desire, need and status. Our demotivators might include cost, effort, time and (perceived) risk.

Motivators can come from many different sources including our previous experiences, any advice we receive, or preconceptions we hold. If you're thinking of buying a new TV, for example, and I tell you how pleased I am with mine because it is 'ultra HD' and the picture is fantastic, you may look for a TV with this feature. But if you read an article claiming that ultra HD TV screens can give you a headache, you might be motivated to choose a TV without this feature instead.

In order to help prospective clients decide to buy your services, you first need to understand what their motivators are so that you can focus on these (or on dispelling their demotivators) in your marketing and your conversion process. You can even - ethically - install new motivators.

The opportunity to influence a prospective client's existing motivators is critical because these may not be a true reflection of their real need for your services. For instance, they may not understand the consequences of not getting your help, or how much better off they'd be *with* rather than *without* it.

Say, for example, a prospective client is planning to agree a 50/50 split with their spouse on divorce but, without your help, they might lose out on sharing their spouse's pension and thereby not get a true 50/50 split. If you help them understand this, it would greatly increase their motivation to invest in you and your services.

Takeaway: *If you know a prospective client would be better off with your help, increasing their motivation to instruct you is actually the ethical choice.*

Leveraging the buying point

The diagram below illustrates the relationship between cost, desire, and the buying point – the point at which we are motivated to buy something.

The buying point

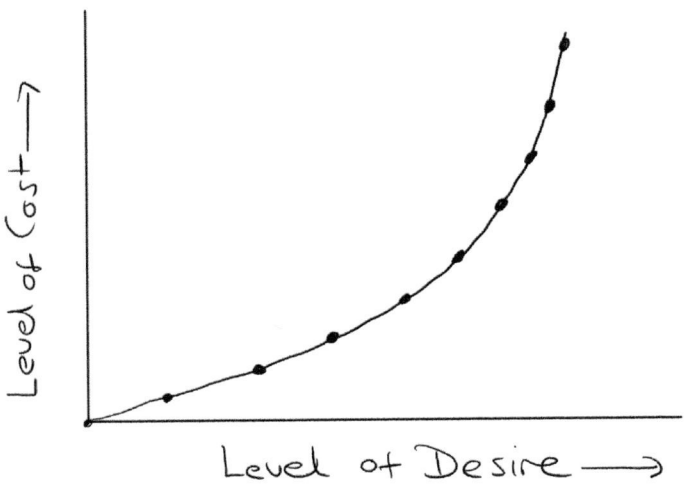

This graph shows how an item with almost zero cost requires us to have very little desire before we buy. But as the cost rises, a higher level of desire (or need) is required.

In addition, this isn't a straight-line increase – because the greater our desire, the more we're prepared to pay in relative terms. This means that once our desire is high enough, we might pay twice as much for an item or service compared with one for which we have only a moderately high level of desire.

If, therefore, you want to overcome any cost objections and be able to charge the fees you want, you need to make sure that the client *strongly* desires what you're offering. To do this, you need to *educate* them about the benefits of having your service - or the consequences of *not* having it. Until they understand this they're simply not able to make a properly informed decision.

Remember, this isn't about selling. It's about exploring and helping them discover their true level of motivation, based on all the facts.

So, before you create your first piece of marketing, you need to understand your ideal clients' motivators and demotivators - so you can gauge their likely buying point. You can then use this information when considering the content of your marketing.

Action Steps:

1. Make a list of the benefits of your service to one specific type of client. Think about these from their point of view. How will they be better off with your help? What pitfalls will you help them avoid? What are the consequences of these pitfalls in time, money, and risk?

   You can download a checklist of possible benefits at www.clientmagnetformula.com

   Keep this list to hand as you go through the rest of this book – we'll be referring back to it.

2. Write down some – real or illustrative – examples of how clients who didn't receive the right help ran into problems, or how your help avoided them doing so. Be *specific* about the consequences of these problems (time, money, risk). These examples will help to support the benefits of your services by showing real world application.

Principle 3: Address the three Cs that are the enemies of marketing

One of the biggest challenges with marketing is persuading your target clients to react to it. If your marketing doesn't stand out, they won't even notice it, never mind absorb the message it contains.

This applies whether you're printing and distributing leaflets, writing website copy, giving talks, chatting to people at networking events, or using social media. In each case you need to find a way to make your marketing stand out. The three main enemies of doing so are: clutter, competition, and caution.

1. **Clutter – it's crowded out there**

From the time we get up until the time we go to bed, we're subjected to a near endless stream of marketing – from adverts on public transport and in the press to social media posts and radio or TV ads.

This means that your marketing isn't just competing with your competitors, it's competing with everyone else out there – whatever the products and services they're promoting.

If your marketing fails to stand out, it'll simply be lost in the crowd.

2. **Competition – why should I choose you?**

Most law firms face an army of competitors, and it's often not clear to clients why they should instruct you rather than one of them.

If your clients don't know why they should choose you, it's probably because you haven't told them. And if you haven't, is it because you aren't sure either?

Unless you communicate this 'why', clients are just as likely to choose one of your competitors rather than you.

3. **Caution – does your marketing follow the crowd?**

Many lawyers don't want to stand out. In fact, because they worry that this might be seen as unprofessional, they tend to be ultra-cautious in their marketing and simply copy what others are doing.

This certainly offends no-one, but neither does it really appeal to anyone.

If you've had any training in marketing, you might have heard: *"You should develop a USP (Unique Selling Proposition) to make you stand out."* In my experience, however, it's quite hard to apply this to a professional services firm. How can you really say that you're unique? You might talk about how long you've been in business, or any accolades you've won, but do clients really care about this? Does it really make you stand out in their eyes?

So what's the solution? The first step is to stop focusing on you and to start focusing on your ideal client – specifically on what their problems might be and how you can help them solve these, or how you can help them achieve a particular goal.

Next, think about how you might best communicate not only that you can help, but that you genuinely understand your ideal clients' concerns, frustrations, hopes and fears. Show them that you see them as real people; remember, even a corporate client is still a person.

Finally, make sure you include all of this in your marketing.

Action Steps:
1. Take the you/we test: Look at all your advertising and marketing – including your website, brochures, and leaflets – and count how many times it uses "I" or "we" rather than "you."
2. This is a really good test of whether your focus is on you or on clients. You should aim for at least two "you's" for every "I" or "we".

Principle 4: Stop ignoring 97% of your ideal clients

Without realising it, most lawyers target only a fraction of their ideal clients with their marketing.

Generally, only a very small percentage of potential clients are actively looking to buy your services right now – whether that's searching on the internet or in directories, or asking friends and family for recommendations.

In fact, most marketing experts quote an average of just 3% of potential clients across all sectors are actively looking for a particular service or product. This means that up to 97% of your ideal clients are *not* actively looking for your services at the moment.

If you're not convinced by this figure as a rule of thumb, test it. Think about all the people you know – friends, family and colleagues (rather than clients) – and consider how many of them are currently *actively* searching for a particular type of lawyer, accountant, or even a new car. It's probably not more than 3%.

The big problem, then, is that most marketing ignores 97% of ideal clients because it only targets the 3% who are actively looking to buy *right now*. It effectively just says *"Here I am, and here's what I do. Would you like to choose me?"*

This kind of 'here I am' marketing is only of interest to someone who's already looking for your services. It doesn't speak to those who might instruct you if they were:

- made aware that they have a problem or need – and that you can solve or provide this; and

- motivated to act now – rather than waiting until it becomes more urgent or pressing.

And if you're thinking, *"If they need my services, why wouldn't they be looking already?"* here are a number of reasons:

- they might not realise the advantage of doing something about their problem *now*, rather than *later*

- they might not understand the consequences of delay

- they might not understand that their problem needs expert help – many people who could be helped by legal advice don't know it

- they might not even know you can help them prevent a problem or achieve a goal – in which case they *definitely* won't be looking for you.

If your marketing can attract just some of these extra potential clients, then it will be considerably more effective then most 'here I am' marketing.

What percentage of your target market are you reaching?

Let's take an example and apply these principles to will writing. Most marketing experts would agree it's likely that:

- Just 3% of your target market are *actively looking* for help to write their will right now.

- 7% of your target market are *open* to help, but aren't currently searching for it. If, however, they saw your marketing it might remind them that it's on their to-do list, and a special offer might prompt them into taking action. But without a reason to call you *now*, they're unlikely to respond.

- A substantial percentage (30%) are *aware* they might need help at some point in the future, but it's not yet on their to-do list. They don't understand *why* it's so important to do it now. Because they're not aware of the risks of waiting, even a special offer is unlikely to spur them into action.

- Another 30% are utterly *unaware* of their problem and how you can help. Imagine, say, a couple who have got married since writing their last will and who don't know that doing so has probably revoked their previous wills. If one of them dies, this could mean that the surviving spouse is only entitled to what they would get under the intestacy rules, i.e. a share of – rather than the full – estate. So even if they see your 'here I am' marketing or hear you introduce yourself at an event as a will writer, they're very unlikely to approach you.

- Finally, 30% will never buy from you. Either you're too far away, too expensive, or they simply don't like you! But ignoring this 30% allows you to focus on the 70% who – with the right information – could be motivated to start actively looking for your help.

Your target market

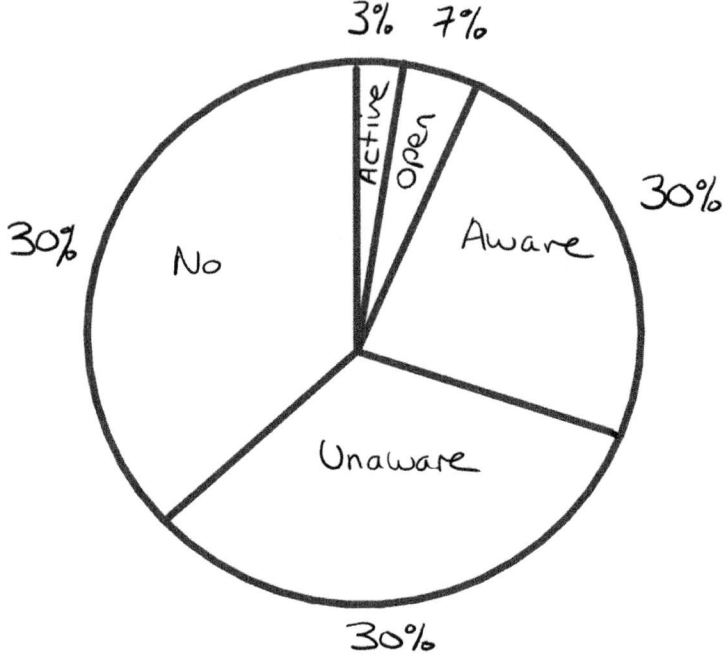

I'm sure you can see how this knowledge offers you a huge opportunity. With some simple changes, your existing marketing could easily reach at least ten times the number of potential clients.

And what would the result be for your practice in client numbers and fee income if your marketing could reach 30%, 50%, or even 67% more of your ideal clients?

Principle 5: Educate your ideal clients about "why"

Educating a prospective client about *why* they need to take action or *how* you can help them is probably something you do without thinking during their initial consultation.

But having got this far, you'll realise that this consultation is only likely to take place if they were already actively looking for help – which leaves a large percentage of people who you'll never get a chance to explain it to.

What if your marketing could do this educating for you, before you even meet with a prospective client?

And what if, instead of 'here I am' marketing, you used a different type? One that positioned you as the expert, rather than simply another seller?

Education-Based Marketing does just that. It allows you to educate prospective clients about their problems and the solutions you can provide. It not only helps them understand why they need your services (and why *now*), but it also provides valuable information *and* initiates a relationship with your prospective clients, both of which make them more likely to decide to instruct you.

By focusing on your clients' needs rather than your credentials, it helps you stand out – because you're doing something different, whilst remaining completely professional. After all, educating clients about how you can help them or the consequences of the situation they are in is a core part of what you do as a lawyer. But we're now talking about your marketing doing that too.

Education-Based Marketing can take many forms, from a free report on a particular topic to a video or a series of tips circulated by email. Or, at a more advanced level, it might be webinar training or a seminar. In fact, it can be anything that will educate your ideal clients.

Case Study: From marketing to 3% to reaching 70%

Here's an illustration of just how big a difference Education-Based Marketing can make. One of my clients, Avril, is a costs lawyer. Her areas of expertise include helping solicitors prepare their bill of costs at the end of an action, but she can also help them in many other ways.

If, for example, she's instructed early enough, she can regularly review the solicitor's files to make sure they've correctly recorded all their time. This not only ensures they can bill their client correctly, but it also allows them to include this figure in any costs they're able to claim from the other side.

Although Avril saved one of her clients £30,000 by doing this, many solicitors don't hire a cost lawyer until the end of an action – either because they don't realise they have a problem, or they don't realise how someone like Avril could help. But Avril's marketing didn't help them understand this – it was 'here I am' marketing that just said she offered 'costs' services to lawyers.

That's why, when she joined my *5 Step Client Attraction Programme*, I helped Avril to change her marketing so that it educated all her ideal clients on how they could save thousands of pounds – simply by instructing her earlier. As a result of this change, her marketing was able to target a much bigger percentage of her ideal clients (up to 70%) rather than just the small percentage who were already looking for a costs lawyer.

Action Steps:

1. Do you remember how earlier I said that *you* were the expert in knowing what clients need to know before they understand why they need your services? Well it's time to get that expertise out of your head and on to paper.

   Start by answering: *What is the one thing that – if my ideal client knew it – would convince them to instruct me today?*

   To help, you can download my 'Client Hook' worksheet that will help you identify this 'one thing' for a situation a typical client is facing where they need your help. Download it here: <u>www. clientmagnetformula.com</u>

2. If you're finding this exercise difficult then make a list of:

   - The pitfalls or challenges they need to overcome.
   - The consequences of getting it wrong (or of not getting it right).
   - What might happen if they tried to do it without your help?
   - How they'd be better off with your help.
   - How they'd benefit from taking action *now*.
   - Why it would be better to choose you rather than one of your competitors.

   Review this list to see which is the most important thing for your ideal client to know so that they want to instruct you now?

Principle 6: Accept that marketing is like dating – you need to develop a relationship before asking for commitment

Have you heard the expression *"People buy from people they know, like, and trust"*?

In the past, simply being a professional might have given you enough standing to be trusted by clients even before they'd met you. But times have changed. With increased competition, clients are increasingly choosy about who they give their business to, and this trust has to be earned.

True, not all prospective clients feel they need to get to know you first – perhaps you've been recommended, or you have an excellent reputation in your field – but what about all the others? Unless you take time to build a relationship with them, they're less likely to choose to work with you.

The best way to start this relationship is through marketing that allows you to give value and build trust – rather than marketing that asks them to call you immediately.

Don't expect a kiss on the first date

In many ways, marketing is just like dating. It's about not asking for a kiss before the first date. (Unless, that is, you're prepared for a rather abrupt refusal!)

That's why marketing needs to be a step-by-step relationship building system – one which warms up your ideal client until they're ready to say "yes" to working with you.

Education-Based Marketing, done well, provides value *and* starts to develop a relationship of trust between you and your ideal clients. But to maximise this you need to follow up and keep the relationship warm. This makes it essential to use your marketing to collect contact details and get permission to stay in touch.

Principle 7: Use a Client Magnet report or guide

Once you've decided what your ideal clients need to know if they're to understand why they need your service – and why they should choose you – you need to deliver this information.

This is where I recommend using a Client Magnet – Education-Based Marketing in the form of a report, guide, checklist or video that you can give to potential clients (you'll find some great examples on the Resources page of my website: www.thebusinessinstructor.com). It's your delivery vehicle and is specifically designed to attract clients *to* you – just like a magnet attracts iron filings.

Why do you need a delivery vehicle for your Education-Based Marketing?

Although – by giving value – Education-Based Marketing can start a relationship, to be successful this relationship must be *ongoing* if prospective clients are to take the next step and contact you.

If they visit your website, for example, and find the information they're looking for without providing their contact details, obviously you can't follow up. There's no opportunity to stay in touch, to send more information, or to ask if you can help in another way.

One way to initiate this conversation is by including your Education-Based Marketing in a free report which you send after prospective clients provide an email or postal address.

Studies reveal that, on average, it takes seven points of contact before we commit to doing business with somebody for a high value service. Relying on one (such as a website visit), but without a way to follow this up, will only result in instructions from a tiny percentage of potential clients. You'll miss out on all those who might have instructed you had you taken more time to develop a relationship with them.

Start with a free report or guide

Free reports or guides are not only the easiest for you to create, they're also the easiest for potential clients to say "yes" to. A report can be read at any time, whereas a training event requires them to be available at a specific time on a specific date. (Webinars and seminars are often an effective second step in your Education-Based Marketing strategy.)

Once you have the details of a prospective client, you can follow up with *relevant* material, questions and conversations. At the most basic level, this might simply be, *"Did you receive it?"* However, you can also invite them to take the next step, which might be to meet. Or – as long as your report has educated them sufficiently about why they need you – they'll approach you when they're ready.

Success Tip

There's no such thing as a one-size-fits-all Client Magnet. Unless you only help one type of client with one type of problem, you'll need a different Client Magnet for each. But start with one and get that working first. You can then repeat the process for other client types or services.

The success of your Client Magnet depends on it being focused enough to appeal to your target clients, but not so focused that its market becomes too small. One of my most successful Client Magnets, for example, is 'The 3 Biggest Mistakes That Keep Most Solicitors From Attracting Enough Clients (And How To Fix Them in 90 Days)'. This targets a group of my ideal clients (solicitors) with a problem I know I can help them with (marketing), but it's also an audience I know is quite large.

Why a Client Magnet is the cornerstone of your Client Attraction Formula

- By explaining the problems prospective clients may have, or their consequences, it provides value and begins a relationship of 'know, like, trust'. (Contrast this with simply asking a client to instruct you on day one.)

- Telling clients how to get more help from you gives you the chance to develop this relationship. (You aren't asking them to say "yes" after the first date at the risk of never seeing them again.)

- Done well, Client Magnets will position you as an expert, rather than as a salesperson.

- Having your information to hand makes it less likely that potential clients will look elsewhere.

- Gaining their contact details allows you to follow up and encourage them towards taking the next step of becoming a client.

Principle 8: Make sure your Client Magnet attracts, not repels

In my *5 Step Client Attraction Programme*, I teach my clients the six elements that are critical to creating a successful Client Magnet.

The most important of these is to make sure you give the *right amount* of value. I find giving too much is a major problem for lawyers who are already using some form of Education-Based Marketing.

The problem with giving too much value is that instead of attracting clients, you repel them. After reading your Client Magnet they think they already know everything and no longer need you.

To illustrate, let me tell you about one of my clients, Andrew. Andrew was frustrated because, despite a large number of articles on his website, he wasn't getting the number of client enquiries he'd hoped for. When I saw his website content, I realised potential clients could visit his site, read what they needed, download some tips and advice, and then leave. He was giving away so much that they didn't think they needed any more from him.

Once I'd helped him to become more strategic about the kinds of articles he wrote, his enquiries increased by a third. He said:

*"I can already see a significant increase in the number of new enquiries, and the percentage who become clients. **In the first 6 months of this year, enquiries have increased by 30% and the percentage of those enquiries becoming clients has increased by 36%.**"*

This highlights the difference between *information* and *Education-Based Marketing*. While information is facts, figures, content and so on that might answer a prospective client's questions, Education-Based Marketing is the *right kind* of information, presented in the *right way*. It should help your ideal client understand *why* they need your service, *why* they should choose *you* to provide it, and *why* they should get your help *now*.

The right information ensures that a prospective client wants more help, not less.

Success Tip

As well as educating your ideal clients about why they need your help, your Client Magnet needs to invite your ideal clients to take the next step – typically an initial consultation (whether free or paid). If you don't make this clear, you might end up educating them about why they need help, only for them to get it from someone else. (For more information on how to run these initial consultations, see Chapters 6 and 7.)

Principle 9: Make sure you're in pole position

Unless they've received a specific recommendation from someone they trust, most people have little idea how to choose one lawyer over another.

In fact, without guidance, they're as likely to base this decision on whichever website they found easiest to use, or whether they liked your receptionist.

This offers the ideal opportunity to educate prospective clients about what 'buying criteria' they should use. In other words, the facts, figures and information they should take into account when choosing a lawyer. If you can include this subtly in your marketing *and* in your subsequent conversations with them, then you can influence – ethically – how they make that choice.

You might, for example, need to help clients understand what to look for when choosing a divorce lawyer. Is membership of certain associations important? Or is it more important to look for one who practices collaborative law or who has a good record on mediated settlements?

Once you've successfully explored together what's most important *for them*, the chances are that they'll look for someone who possesses exactly those qualities. If, therefore, you can demonstrate that you do, it's likely they'll consider choosing you.

Action Steps:

1. Make a list of the reasons why prospective clients should choose you rather than a competitor. These are the 'buying criteria' you want to educate your ideal clients about.

    *   Remember, your competitors include alternative service providers or DIY options as well as other lawyers.
    *   Think about these reasons from a client's point of view – do they really care about how long established you are or the awards you've won?

2. Make a list of any possible objections to hiring you. (Ignore these at your peril – you'll need to overcome them before prospective clients will say "yes" to working with you.)

    Keep your list of 'buying criteria' and possible objections to hand as you go through the rest of this book – we'll be referring back to them.

Chapter 5
Putting The Principles Into Action With The 5 Step Client Attraction System

After reading the previous chapter, you should now understand the importance of using Education-Based Marketing in the form of a Client Magnet. If so, then it's time to introduce an overview of my 5 Step Client Attraction System. I teach this to my clients so they can plan, create, and use a Client Magnet to attract their ideal clients in a consistent and predictable way.

Step 1: Create a blueprint

You wouldn't start building a house without first planning what you wanted it to look like, would you? The same applies to building a Client Magnet. Unless you start with the right blueprint, you could end up wasting a lot of time, effort and money creating something that doesn't bring the results you want.

To create your blueprint, you must start by identifying what your ideal clients need to understand before they agree to instruct you. You then need to decide the best way to communicate this, so that they understand *why* they need your solution and *why* they should choose *you*.

The good news is you've already started to build your blueprint through the action steps in Chapter 4. If you've completed these action steps then you already know:

- Your target for the next 90 days (your ideal clients and the service you want to provide to them).

- How you can help them achieve a goal, or overcome a problem.

- The areas you need to educate them about to convince them why they want/need your services (the benefits they'd gain, or the pitfalls they'd avoid).

- How you can educate them on these (perhaps case studies or examples that explain the consequences if they do/don't take up your services).

- Why they should choose you rather than a competitor for this specific type of work.

Action Steps:

1. Download a copy of the Education-Based Marketing Blueprint Planning Tool I give clients who are implementing my 5 Step Client Attraction System from www.clientmagnetformula.com

2. Complete the Education-Based Marketing Blueprint using the information you've already assembled from the action steps in Chapter 4.

Step 2: Create your Client Magnet

The next step is to create the content for your Client Magnet. To do this, you need to combine the right *ingredients* (information) with the right *recipe* (structure).

Remember: Client Magnets must be client-focused and avoid giving away so much information that potential clients think they no longer need your help. Here are my top tips for creating effective and successful Client Magnets:

Use an attention-grabbing title

Without a must-read title, your Client Magnet simply won't be read. Titles that work best:

- identify a problem and how clients can avoid or solve it ('7 Strategies to Reduce…..'); or

- promise a benefit or a solution ('5 Steps to [result] without [risk]'); or

- use intrigue to arouse curiosity (5 Secrets to [result]' or '5 Things You Need to Know Before You [take this step]').

Don't worry about being perfect

Writing the content of their first Client Magnet is where many lawyers get bogged down. Often this is because they don't have a clear enough plan (see Step 1) or, if this kind of writing is new to them, they get stuck worrying about the need to be perfect.

To illustrate this, one of my clients, Lucy, was convinced she had no talent for writing 'this kind of thing'. But by simply following the templates and guidance I provide in my *5 Step Client Attraction Programme*, the very first

Client Magnet report she wrote won her a meeting with a major new client who hired her on the spot.

Provide education *not* information

As part of my Client Attraction System I give all my clients in-depth training on my '6 Part Rapid Content Formula', which makes writing the content of Client Magnets easy and effective. It sets out exactly what content to include – as well as what *not* to include – and in which order.

A core part of this is ensuring you show the value of your service for each specific client, which you can do by following these steps:

   a. **Educate** your ideal clients on:

       i.   problems they don't know they have; or

       ii. the impact/consequences of problems they know they have; or

       iii. how someone like you can provide a solution to these problems; and

   b. **Explain** the solution you offer, or provide tips to avoid the problem.

Using this formula will help you quickly turn *information* into *Education-Based Marketing*.

Educate your ideal clients on problems they don't know they have

If your ideal client doesn't yet know they have a problem, your Client Magnet must educate them about its existence before it can hope to educate them about its impact or consequences – or the fact that you can help them solve it.

To give an example, people often only go to a family lawyer when a crisis, such as divorce, happens. Sadly, they rarely think about putting legal safeguards in place *before* things go wrong. Yet, in the case of unmarried couples, a co-habitation agreement could prevent disputes if they later split up.

To realise they need this service, potential clients need to know:

- Firstly – because they don't have the same rights as married couples – there could be problems if they split up.

- Secondly, they can protect themselves – should this situation arise – by having an agreement in place setting out how things would be divided. (It may require a small investment now, but it's much less expensive than trying to sort out any problems later in court.)

After all, no one buys a solution to a problem they don't know they have, so simply marketing co-habitation agreements without this explanation is very unlikely to work.

Demonstrate impact and consequences

Unless you show the significance of these consequences, they won't act as a buying motivator. If possible, illustrate your explanation with real-life examples or case studies. This will not only add credibility, it'll also help clients to better understand the consequences. (Most of us learn more effectively from stories than we do from facts or unsubstantiated assertions.)

Show the gap

Never leave the reader thinking they know so much that they no longer need your help. Reminding them about problems they still have, or why they might need more help – without coming across as overly pushy or too eager to sell your services – is part of the fine balancing act required to create a successful Client Magnet.

Position yourself as the expert of choice

There's little point in educating clients about why they need expert help, only to have them instruct one of your competitors instead.

That's why you should refer back to your list of 'Why Choose Me?' reasons from Chapter 4. It'll remind you about what prospective clients need to know before they understand why they should choose you – your positive attributes, and how you can overcome any objections they may have.

Takeaway: *Make sure you have all the ingredients for your Client Magnet in place before you start writing. Then follow a proven recipe.*

Step 3: Make a compelling next-step invitation

What do you want clients to do once they've read your report or guide and realised they need your help? It'll be just so much wasted time and effort if they're not sure what to do next, or if the next step is too big because, either way, they're unlikely to take action.

Consider this in the context of the specific client your Client Magnet is targeting. What kind of next-step invitation will motivate them, and what won't? And which type will work best for your particular practice?

Expecting – or asking – prospective clients to instruct you immediately after reading your Client Magnet report is a little like proposing marriage on a first date. Most are unlikely to be ready for that. But just providing your Education-Based Marketing content and hoping they'll take action rarely works either.

An appropriate next-step invitation might be to offer them a consultation (either free, or paid) at which you review their situation and help them see where they need help. (Remember though, to maximise your chances of being instructed, don't give away too much information in this initial meeting. See Chapter 6 for more detail.)

Another option might be to invite them to an event, or to encourage them to ask for more information – whatever's most likely to move them closer to becoming a paying client. Whichever you choose, make sure you give a compelling reason why they should take this next step.

Andrew – the commercial lawyer I've already mentioned – was really struggling with this before we started working together. Using lots of articles to market his services, but without any next-step invitations, meant he didn't really have a strategy beyond, *"Give them value and hope it'll mean they instruct me."* Hope is not a strategy! With my help, however, introducing a clear next-step invitation to a specific consultation related to the Client Magnet topic helped to increase the number of enquiries he received by 30%.

Once you've decided on the kind of invitation that will most appeal to the readers of your Client Magnet, you need to focus on ways to increase its take-up rate.

Even if you decide on a free consultation, for example, you'll still need to 'sell' it by explaining its benefits and why prospective clients should come. So make sure you name and describe your session in an enticing way. (You may be surprised by how reluctant some people can be to give up their time if they don't understand what's in it for them.)

Success Tip

Many lawyers advertise that they offer free advice in the form of an initial session of 15 or 30 minutes. Although - as it provides an opportunity to start a conversation - this might seem like a good idea, the danger is in the words 'free advice session', which suggests potential clients can ask for advice on whatever they want. Hundreds of lawyers have told me that this often results in the prospective client asking a lot of questions, getting the answers they *think* they need (but don't necessarily) and then not instructing them. So never describe your next-step invitation as a 'free advice session'.

To download a worksheet on how to name and describe your session go to <u>www. clientmagnetformula.com</u>

Step 4: Magnetise your clients

No matter how good your Client Magnet is, unless your ideal clients see it they can't read it or take the next steps.

So which are the best - online and offline - methods of making sure they do? The main points to consider are:

1. How can you use your Client Magnet with **existing clients and prospects** to get more enquiries?

2. How can you work with **existing contacts** – such as other professionals with similar clients – to get your Client Magnet in front of your ideal clients?

3. How can you use your Client Magnet to directly reach completely **new clients**?

4. How can you get **new contacts** – other professionals, organisations or associations – to promote your Client Magnet to their clients?

For each of these, your Client Magnet should form the cornerstone of all your marketing. Instead of 'reinventing the wheel' each time it comes to preparing content, you'll be able to use extracts from it to educate your ideal clients – whether in blogposts, on social media, in newsletters, leaflets or videos. (All of which should entice readers to visit your website and sign up to download the full Client Magnet report.)

In other words, your Client Magnet will actually reduce the amount of time you need to spend on marketing.

Ways of marketing a Client Magnet

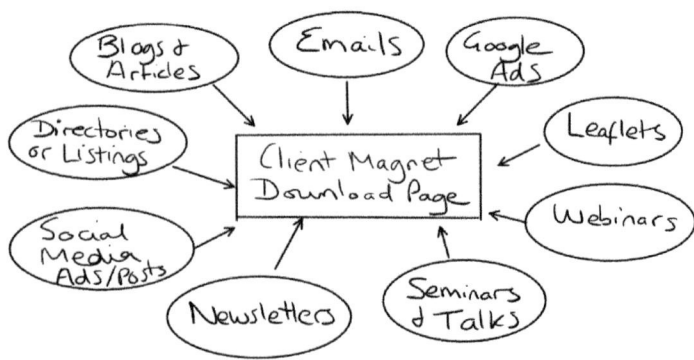

Success Tip

A key step to success is to put your Client Magnet on a webpage, behind a sign-up box. Any visitors who want a copy will have to enter their name and email (or physical) address, plus appropriate permission for you to contact them. This will allow you to start the ongoing relationship that's essential if you want to maximise your results.

Step 5: Start a conversation

This is the final and most important step – because it's about turning views of your Client Magnet into actual meetings with *prospective* clients in which you convince them to become *paying* ones.

As I discussed in Chapter 4, because it takes on average seven points of contact before a client is ready to invest in your services, follow up is critical. But it needs to be done in the right way, with the right combination of the following three elements:

- **Mindset**: Why are you following up, and why is this good for the client?

- **Expert positioning**: How can you retain the expert positioning your Client Magnet has created (and avoid becoming just another salesperson)?

- **Automation**: How can you follow up in a systemised way that brings consistent results *without* taking up more of your time?

Frustratingly, all too many lawyers don't follow up after an initial contact because they don't want to feel pushy or that they're selling something. My *5 Step Client Attraction Programme* helps overcome this because it's based on developing client relationships. Once you find ways to follow up that feel comfortable, professional, *and* which position you as an expert and trusted advisor, you'll discover how much it can actually enhance your client relationships.

Results

Adopting my 5 Step Client Attraction System will quickly help you to achieve bigger and better results, all without having to spend more time on marketing. Yes, you'll need to invest a little time and effort initially, but once it's up and running it'll do the work for you – allowing you to get on with all the other demands of running an increasingly busy practice.

If you adopt this system, then just like Avril the costs lawyer, you could extend the reach of your marketing from 3% to 70%, including those potential clients who don't know they need help or why they need it from someone with your expertise.

Or like Andrew, the commercial lawyer, you could use the principles of my system to increase your enquiries by 30% – with 36% more of these becoming paying clients.

And, if you still need convincing, this is the exact system that enabled me to triple my fee income in year two of my business and which has enabled me to build a business that generates a multiple six figure sum each year.

Further help and resources

Before you start to build your system, make sure you have everything you need to make it work.

Here's a reminder of the key points:

- Are you clear who your target market should be?

- Have you decided which topic will best educate your ideal clients about what they need to understand if they're to want your services?

- Have you created a must-read title?

- Do you know what content to include (and not to include), and in which order?

- Do you have a compelling next-step invitation?

- Are you confident you've developed the necessary skills to implement your marketing plan, including writing the content of web pages, preparing advertising and managing online marketing?

If you'd like more advice on any of these, or would like to further support to develop your skills, then you can find out more about my *5 Step Client Attraction Programme* here: www.profitablelegalpractice.com/attract

This 90 day programme provides ready-to-use templates and in-depth, hands-on training from me on the best way to implement each step of my system, as well as how to tailor it for your specific practice and ideal clients.

CONVERT

Chapter 6
Client Conversion:
9 Key Principles

Assuming you already have enquiries coming into your practice, the easiest way to increase client numbers and improve your profitability is to increase your conversion rate (i.e. your success at turning enquiries into paying clients).

What's your current process for doing this?

Many lawyers offer an initial consultation or advice session - often free - as the first step. The objective of this is to find out whether they can help a particular prospect and, if they can, to persuade the prospect to instruct them.

This session, then, is a conversion tool. It's how you turn an enquiry into a paying client (or into an ongoing paying client if you charge for the initial session).

However, there are a number of steps involved in this process, all of which take time - and therefore cost money.

First, you have to generate interest in your consultation through networking, advertising, writing, speaking, or through getting referrals. Next you need to invite a prospective client to this meeting and, once they've accepted, prepare for it. Then there's the meeting itself and, because they won't necessarily say "yes" straight away, the – perhaps multiple – follow-ups before you get an answer.

How long does this process take – and how much does it cost? Let's look at an example.

If we assume it takes three hours – from first meeting a prospect to their becoming a client – and your success rate is one-in-three (i.e. a 33% conversion rate), then each new client will 'cost' 9 hours to acquire.

In terms of the monetary cost of this, you need to consider two factors: your marketing spend *and* your time spend (in other words, the cost of *not earning* the fees you could have if you'd been working on a client file during that time).

If, say, you're using Google ads to get online enquiries, it might cost you £50 per enquiry but no time. If, however, you're trying to get enquiries through a networking event and it takes two hours to generate each enquiry, the time cost would be £400 (assuming a rate of £200 an hour), plus whatever money you spend to attend the networking event.

To keep it simple, let's assume you spend an average of £100 in time and/or money to get each enquiry. A conversion rate of 33% would mean you'd spend £300 on marketing to gain each new client.

Now let's look at the difference that improving your conversion rate to two-in-three (66%) makes:

Conversion rate	1-in-3 (33%)	2-in-3 (66%)
Total time needed to deal with enquiries to convert one client	9 hours	4.5 hours
Cost (time and money) to generate each enquiry	£300	£150

As this shows, it would halve the time and cost it takes to gain each new client. As a result you could:

1. repurpose the time you save into doing more fee-earning work for existing clients *and* cut down on your marketing expenses – both of which would increase your profits; or

2. keep doing the same amount of marketing and spend the same amount of time in initial consultations, *but get twice as many clients from your efforts* – reducing the cost and increasing the profit from each new client.

This is how better client conversion rates result in more clients and more profit without working more hours.

Before you start

If most of your work comes through recommendations and referrals then you might be thinking, *"My conversion rate is good. I don't need to worry about it."*

This would be a mistake.

Once you start to generate enquiries from beyond these sources, it's likely your conversion rate will drop.

This is normal, because recommendations and referrals will always be the easiest to convert.

In fact, I've seen conversion rates of 80% on such 'warm' enquiries drop to 10% for cold ones – often because the same approach is used for the initial consultation for both.

Remember, you need to adapt your process and develop your skills, which is why I now want to share with you 9 key principles to improve your conversion rate.

Principle 1: Plug the holes in your bucket

If you don't have a reliable system for converting enquiries into paying clients, then you have 'Leaky Bucket Syndrome'.

If you imagine enquiries as being like water flowing from a tap, you need to have a bucket ready to catch (convert) as many as possible. But Leaky Bucket Syndrome means you have holes in your bucket through which these enquiries can escape.

The sooner you fix these holes, the sooner you'll start to get more clients from your current marketing, *and* the sooner you'll stop spending time and money on marketing only to lose these enquiries at the conversion stage.

In addition, once you've plugged the holes, you'll be able to turn the tap on full, confident you're making the most of all the enquiries you receive.

The first step is to identify where the leaks are. Then you can decide how to plug them.

Action Steps:

1. Review your entire conversion process to check for leaks. List all the steps that new enquiries must take between first contact and becoming a client and then work out which has the highest drop-out rate or offers the biggest opportunities if you were to plug the hole.

   You can see examples of steps and processes to consider in my '7 Steps To Client Conversion' checklist at www.clientmagnetformula.com

2. List three to five areas you need to improve, and then prioritise them in the order you want to tackle them.

Success Tip

Initial meetings are a good place to start looking for holes because they normally have the biggest impact on conversion rates.

But look, too, at how prospective clients are treated from the moment they first contact you - whether by email, phone or in person. If this isn't dealt with well, it could deter prospective clients from getting to your initial consultation in the first place.

Principle 2: Don't offer free advice sessions

As I've discussed previously, many lawyers offer some kind of free initial advice. But why?

It's almost certainly not because they want to give their advice away for free.

In most cases, it's a way of talking to prospective clients to discover what their problem is and whether you can help. In any other industry this would be called a sales meeting – a meeting to find out whether what the prospect wants and what you can offer are a good fit.

But the last thing most lawyers want is prospective clients thinking they're coming to a sales meeting, so they call this a free advice session instead. And, invariably, this leaves them stuck in an awkward position.

If you *don't* provide this free advice, the client will be unhappy and won't instruct you.

If you *do* provide it, the client will very likely leave thinking they no longer need your services.

In the second scenario, not only have you given away your time for nothing, but you've actually done the client a *disservice*. Getting the answers they thought they were looking for doesn't mean they'll be able to deal with their problem with the same level of expertise as you.

I'm not saying never offer a *free initial consultation* – but I *am* saying don't base this on giving free advice around the client's agenda or questions.

Action Steps:

1. Refer back to Chapter 5 (Client Attraction System Step 3) and review how you named and described your initial consultation. Make sure it's clear you're not offering free advice. That way, it'll be easier to manage expectations.

2. Replace any reference to 'free advice' on your website or in your marketing with the name of your initial consultation.

Principle 3: Stop 'tap dancing'

As lawyers, because most of us are uncomfortable with selling, we instead try to impress. It's as though we're contestants in a talent show, and prospective clients are the judge. We 'tap dance' furiously, hoping we can impress them enough to win their instructions.

In reality, this often means we try to impress them by showing our expertise in the form of free advice. After all, if we don't want to sell, how else can we persuade them to say "yes"?

But there is an alternative; one which starts with understanding what makes a client want to buy and what they need to know before they'll do so. (I promise it's hardly ever about how impressed they are by your technical knowledge. After all, very few clients are in a position to evaluate this.)

So what you need to do instead is identify their need for your services and then create their desire to buy them. You can do this most easily by following the 5 Step Client Conversion System I'll outline in Chapter 7.

Confessions of a tap dancer

When I first started out I was definitely guilty of tap dancing. I'd spend ages giving prospective clients strategies to grow their business and attract more clients but, ironically, although this brought me lots of praise, it didn't bring me any paying clients.

The truth is I wasn't helping them to understand their underlying problems (or the consequences) which, in virtually every case, were down to the lack of a good sales and marketing system. Although the consequences of not fixing this were many thousands of pounds in missed business, my free advice would instead end up helping them to fix one or two minor problems such as an issue with Google Ads.

When I changed the focus of my initial consultations – from being about free advice to being about identifying their problems and helping them understand why they needed to fix these – my success rate more than doubled.

That's what I want for you, too.

Principle 4: Help clients understand why they need professional help

Before a prospective client will say "yes" to working with you they need to understand:

- why they need your type of professional help and how it'll help them get a better or quicker result; and

- why they should get your help now rather than later. (The idea they can wait is one of your biggest enemies.)

If by now you've prepared your Client Magnet, you should already have addressed these two questions. So, in your initial consultation, you now have the opportunity to make sure your prospective clients really understand these 'whys' and how they apply to their specific situation.

Simply telling them why they'll be better off with your help, could, however, sound pushy or arrogant. Instead, consider how you can ask questions that will help them see this for themselves.

For example, instead of saying: *"Unless you fix this issue, you'll be facing the same problems in 12 months"*, you could ask: *"What will happen if you don't fix this issue – where will you be 12 months from now?"*

If they don't respond with *"I'll be having these same problems"*, you could prompt them by asking: *"Do you think you'll still be facing these same problems?"*

The more you can help prospective clients to hear themselves say that they have a problem – and that it's one which needs fixing – the less convincing you'll need to do. This makes questions one of the most powerful tools available to you during initial consultations.

Action Steps:

1. Refer back to the list of benefits of your services for a specific client (which you created as an action step from Chapter 5, Principle 2). Select three to five facts or risks that they really need to understand if they're to be motivated to get your help.

2. Identify questions you can ask during your initial consultation that will help prospective clients see these facts/risks for themselves. (You can find some good examples in my 'Question-Generator' checklist at www.clientmagnetformula.com)

Success Tip

If a prospective client hasn't already read your Client Magnet, make sure you send them a copy before their initial consultation. That way you can help set the 'buying criteria' for them in advance of your consultation. (Refer back to Chapter 4 for how to set the 'buying criteria'.)

Principle 5: Help clients see the true value of your services

Prospective clients won't buy your services unless they understand their value – which means their value specifically to *them*.

Do you ever reach the end of an initial consultation, after you've given your proposal as to how you can help, only to hear: *"It's too expensive"* or *"I've seen it cheaper somewhere else"*?.

You might be tempted to put this down to competition but, in many cases, the real reason is that we only buy something when our need for it - or its payoff - *is greater than its cost.* If your prospective client doesn't understand how your services will bring them a greater value than they cost, there's very little chance they'll say "yes".

For clients to understand the value of your services, they first need to understand what you'll do for them. But - and this is a really important point - what you'll do *isn't* about drafting an agreement, or making an application to court. Instead, it's about the *end result for them,* which might be:

- achieving a particular goal; or

- eliminating a particular problem; or

- providing peace of mind.

If you describe your services in terms of the hours you spend or the processes you complete, clients will start to focus on whether your fee is worth that per hour or per step. So you need them to focus on the *value* of the result instead.

To do this, emphasise what's in it for them. Help them understand the consequences of not getting your help, or how they'd be better off if they did. For example:

- How could their project be achieved more quickly, cheaply or safely?

- How could they get a result with you that they couldn't on their own?

- How might they avoid a risk by putting in place an agreement or other legal document?

This is all about how you describe the result you'll provide. For example, however good value it may actually represent, if a physiotherapist told you, *"It'll cost you £600 for six 60-minute physio sessions"*, you would probably think, *"£100 per session? That seems a lot. Shouldn't I shop around before I agree?"*

If, however, they said, *"It'll cost you £600 to reduce (or get rid of) your backache – the same backache which prevents you from playing with your kids, makes sitting at a desk uncomfortable, and stops from you sleeping at night"*, most people would be much more likely to part with £600 – or even more – for that.

I'm not suggesting you overinflate fees, but you should set them in the context of how much you'll help your clients. Once you understand how to do this effectively, you'll also be able to increase your prices and still get clients to say "yes".

Action Steps:

1. Decide what your equivalent of curing backache is.

2. Using real-life examples, write down the results your ideal clients could achieve by following your advice – or problems they could avoid.

> **Success Tip**
>
> When you talk to a prospective client, imagine *"What's in it for me?"* is written on their forehead.
>
> Only when you show them that the answer to this is greater than what they have to pay (in time, effort or money) will they say "yes".

Principle 6: Show clients why they should choose you

Once a client has decided they need help, they still need to decide whether they want you – rather than one of your competitors – to provide it.

That's why it's critical to establish trust and rapport during initial consultations by listening, showing interest, and demonstrating that you understand what clients want to achieve.

By itself though, this won't be enough.

At the end of Chapter 4 (Principle 9) we looked at setting the 'buying criteria' for your ideal clients. Let's now refer back to your list of reasons as to why clients should choose you.

Make sure you use this information in your initial consultations. Bring into the conversation the 'buying criteria' you want prospective clients to consider and, at the same time, demonstrate how you fit these. A good way to do this is by giving examples of how you've helped other clients facing similar situations or challenges to theirs.

For example: *"In divorce cases like yours, where the spouse has a high-value pension, it's vital to get the correct valuation of this if you're to get your fair share of the assets. I've helped many clients in exactly this situation, in particular where the initial valuation put forward by the spouse's advisors has been calculated on the wrong basis. By insisting on getting a higher valuation agreed I've often helped clients get a settlement that's £100,000-£200,000 higher."*

From the same action step in Chapter 4, you should also have a list of possible objections to engaging your services. Keep these in mind, too, and find ways to address them. For example, if a prospective client thinks your firm is too small, show them why a small firm is actually the best choice in their situation (perhaps because they will get more personal attention).

Principle 7: Talk less, question more

So far, we've focused on what prospective clients need to understand during your conversion process, including:

- why they need or should want your services

- why you're the right person to provide these services

- why they should take action now rather than later

- why your services are good value.

Because *telling* can very easily come across as *selling*, I teach clients in my *5 Step Client Conversion Programme* how to use questions to help prospective clients work out and understand the answers for themselves. Key to this is the need to talk less and listen more.

A good rule of thumb – if you want to ask good questions and fully listen to the answers – is to spend only around 25% of your time during a consultation speaking.

In fact, in the early part of a consultation, while you're finding out about your prospective client's goals and challenges, you might talk as little as 10%.

Later, when you're diagnosing problems and making recommendations, you'll speak more. But even then, the more you use questions to help clients see the value and relevance of your suggestions, the more likely they'll accept them.

Action Steps:

1. Consider three of your most recent initial consultations with prospective clients. Who did most of the talking?

2. If you spoke for more than 25% of the time, at which points could you have asked more questions and listened to their answers instead?

3. Make a list of the additional questions you would ask next time.

Principle 8: Use the 'Conversation that Converts' framework

There are three phases to successful conversion:

Let's look at each in turn:

Goals: The first phase is to discover prospective clients' real goals or needs. Do they want to achieve a specific outcome? Or avoid a particular problem?

Too often we tell clients what we can do for them *before* we find out enough information about what they really want. That's why it's so important to ask open questions (rather than ones that prompt a "yes" or "no" answer) *and* to listen carefully to the answers.

Once you know what your prospective clients want – and why – you can judge whether they'll be a good fit for your services and, if so, how you can best help them. You'll also know what's most likely to motivate them to buy your services – because you'll understand what's important to them.

Challenges: The second phase is to show them *why* they need help (so they recognise they need your services) but *not* how to do it themselves.

To do this, you'll need to help them understand what might stop them from reaching their goals. Helping them to uncover the challenges they face is the best way to ensure they understand how they'd benefit from your advice and support.

Again, asking clear and focused questions – and listening carefully to the answers – is your secret weapon here. Instead of simply telling prospective clients they need your services, try asking them what *they* think they need in order to achieve their goal or to avoid a particular problem. Then listen out for the specific ways you'll be able to help.

Only when you show them the value of getting your help – whether that's achieving something they couldn't on their own, or simply achieving it more cheaply, more quickly, or with less stress - will they be prepared to invest their time/money/effort in your services.

Solution: Finally, after you've listened to everything they've said in phases 1 and 2, remember to explain - with reference to their specific needs - how your services will help them to achieve their goals.

This may sound simple, but it's where many professionals fall down. It's easy to get carried away promoting our own services rather than making sure a client understands why they're right for them. And remember to focus on the *outcome* of your help, rather than the logistics of *how* you'll help.

Action Steps:

1. Use a framework template or prompter during initial consultations to help guide you through these three phases. (You can download an example at www.clientmagnetformula.com)

2. Before your next conversation with a prospective client, prepare a list of key questions that will help them uncover the challenges they face and appreciate the benefits of getting your help.

Success Tip

Approach consultations as if you were a medical specialist. When you first see a medical specialist, they will ask a series of questions, and will listen carefully to your current situation (your challenges) and what you want to be different (your goals). Only then will they give you a prescription (the solution) – for example, pills, surgery or further tests and investigations.

A good doctor won't tell you what you need before they hear your symptoms and understand what you'd like to improve. So why would a good lawyer try to sell their services before finding out what the prospective client really wants and needs?

Principle 9: Follow a system

Have you ever noticed that some consultations go well while others don't?

It's one thing to know you need to help prospective clients understand why they should say "yes" to instructing you. But it's quite another to do it well *every time*.

The only way to guarantee consistent results is to find a process that works and then be able to repeat it. This means creating a system – such as a questionnaire, checklist, or process map – and sticking to it.

Which is why, in the next chapter, I'm going to outline the steps I recommend you take to create one that works for you.

CHAPTER 7
PUTTING THE PRINCIPLES INTO ACTION WITH THE 5 STEP CLIENT CONVERSION SYSTEM

In this chapter I want to show you, step-by-step, how to build your own system for promoting, running, and following up on initial consultations with prospective clients.

There are five steps to creating the most effective system. By following these steps you will increase your conversion rate (and the fees you are able to charge) by:

- positioning yourself as an expert, not a seller

- diagnosing your prospective clients' needs and helping them understand what they really want

- prescribing a solution they actually want (and will invest in)

- helping them understand why they should say "yes" *now*.

Step 1: Prepare

Before you start any consultation or meeting, you must be absolutely clear about what your prospective client has to understand by the end of it if they're to say "yes" to working with you.

As we've already covered, it's important to consider what will motivate them to want your services. What are their fears, or the frustrations they want to avoid? What are the results and benefits they want to achieve? What do they need to understand about you, your services, and the way you work, in order to want to instruct you? This is going to vary from client to client, depending on their individual circumstances, but you should be able to identify some common themes which will apply to many of your ideal clients who are looking for help in a specific area.

Once you've spent some time getting clear on the answers to these questions, you'll know the issues you need to address. You can then ensure that, by the end of your conversation, your prospective clients understand why they need your services (and how they'll benefit), and why they should choose you rather than one of your competitors.

It's essential you get your preparation right – everything which follows depends on it.

Action Steps:

1. Prepare a list of topics or issues to cover in your next consultation to help your prospective clients understand why they should instruct you.

2. Use this list to help you complete the Initial Consultation Planning worksheet available at www.clientmagnetformula.com

---

Step 2: Position

What you do before, during, and after your initial meeting will affect what prospective clients expect from it and how they respond.

Positioning is about getting them to see you, the meeting, and their role in this meeting in a specific way. In this case, the positioning you need to create is that you are the expert, you are in control of the meeting, and they can trust the recommendations you'll make.

The right positioning is key if you're to obtain the right outcome. There are three areas to focus on:

1. Position the initial consultation

How you describe the initial consultation and the benefits a prospective client will gain from it is crucial, because it sets up the expectation of what you'll cover and the outcome they can expect. (Remember: this should *never* be that they'll get free advice.)

Action Steps:
1. Prepare an agenda for your meeting. Use the 'Conversations that Convert' framework outlined in Chapter 6 to help you.   2. List the benefits or results a prospective client will gain from your initial consultation so that you can explain these easily in the first few minutes.

2. Position yourself as an expert

The obvious way to position yourself as an expert is to provide prospective clients with a copy of your Client Magnet that contains advice on the relevant topic. (You can do this in advance of the consultation.)

By itself, however, this is unlikely to be enough. You also need to show you're an expert in helping clients identify the problems or challenges they might be facing and their options for overcoming these.

In other words, showing you're an expert not only *in* the law, but *in applying it to their specific circumstances.*

Success Tip
Remember not to fall into the trap of giving away your advice for free. In the initial meeting you need to demonstrate your expertise in *diagnosing* a client's problem and helping them understand you have the solution.   It's *never* about giving the 'how to' of that solution away for free.

3. Position prospective clients as followers

Have you ever had a prospective client try to run the initial consultation? One who asks questions, demands answers, and leaves you feeling on the back foot?

The best way to avoid this is by positioning yourself as the leader from the beginning.

The way you start your meeting (particularly the first five minutes) is crucial. By making it clear that you'll be the one asking the questions, you'll naturally position clients as the ones who'll be responding. In other words: you ask, they answer. You lead, they follow.

To do this, start by introducing the agenda and how you'll conduct the consultation. Explain that you'll be asking questions and that you'll focus on specific topics in a specific order.

Next, ask if they agree. They almost always will - and, if they don't, it's probably an early indication that they won't be an ideal client.

If they do agree, the good news is that they'll now be ready to follow you, which means you're more likely to be able to lead them towards accepting the solution you recommend.

Action Steps:

1. Create a template script for the first five minutes of your initial consultations.

2. Use it at the next opportunity, and notice the difference it makes to the way you're able to control meetings.

Step 3: Diagnose

This is about uncovering your prospective clients' specific needs or problems (their goals), and what's stopping them (their challenges) from achieving these. You can then ensure you make the right recommendation to help them overcome these (the solution).

Here are some powerful questions you can use to help you:

1. What do they want to achieve? What goal do they have, or what problem do they need to overcome?

2. What's stopping them from achieving this or fixing the problem?

3. What's the gap between where they are now and where they want to be? (This will tell you how big or important their need is.)

Asking the above questions will not only mean you find the answers out for yourself, but it'll also help prospective clients be clear on what they want, how important it is to them, and the sort of help they'll need to achieve it. At this point, they'll be ready to listen to the solution you recommend.

Remember, if you fail to ask the right questions now, you're more likely to get pushback and objections later.

> ### Action Steps:
>
> 1. Make a list of questions to ask during initial consultations that will identify a prospective client's goals and challenges. Remember, these need to encourage people to see the importance *to them* of achieving their goal or fixing a problem. (This will make it easier for them to understand the value of your solution.)
>
> 2. To help get you started, download my Question Generator worksheet at: <u>www. clientmagnetformula.com</u>

Step 4: Prescribe

Once you've correctly diagnosed the needs or problems of your prospective client, you're ready to deliver (prescribe) your recommended solution.

However, a mistake I often see at this point is a professional jumping straight in with details of *how* they'll help with a problem or goal without stopping to explain *why* the client has that problem and *what* they need to do about it.

Imagine if a doctor gave you a prescription for chest pains and simply said, *"Take this twice a day and call me in two weeks."* Unless they first explained why you needed it or how it could help, it wouldn't exactly fill you with confidence, would it?

Similarly, if you want a prospective client to agree to instruct you, you need to explain the 'why', the 'what' and the 'how' of your solution together with the way in which it will help them.

In my *5 Step Client Conversion Programme* I teach a specific formula for delivering your recommendation, where the 'why' and the 'what' always come before the 'how'. That way, your prospective clients will understand exactly *what* your recommendation will do for them, *how* it will help, and *why* they should invest in it.

Here's an overview of that formula:

- **Why**: this is the underlying cause of your client's problem or the pitfall they'll face if they don't solve it. In other words, *why they need your help*.

- **What**: this is the outcome they want or need. For example, if a prospective client's goal is to sell their company quickly, without retaining any ongoing liability, then *why* they need your help is to avoid the factors that can slow down a sale or result in ongoing liabilities. *What* they need is the right preparation to be done pre-sale (to avoid delays), and strong legal protection to be put in place (to limit ongoing liability).

- **How**: this is about the steps they need to take (with your help). For example, it might be how they can prepare for a quick sale (putting in place missing legal documents, or tidying up other internal affairs) or how they can reduce future liability on the sale of their business (by carefully negotiating the company sale documents, ensuring full disclosure and using strong disclaimers). Note: this is not the detailed 'how-to' but instead the general principles.

Action Steps:

1. Write down the 'why', 'what', and 'how' that you want to explain to a specific prospective client in an upcoming consultation you have arranged. Practise saying it out loud so you get used to hearing yourself describe this process.

2. Create a checklist or prompter to help you follow these steps in the right order when you are in your consultations. To give you a starting point, download an overview of my '5 Ps' process for delivering this recommendation at www.clientmagnetformula.com. It will show you the 'Prescribe' process I teach in my *5 Step Client Conversion Programme*.

Success Tip

Make sure you give your prescription (solution) one pill at a time. If you confuse or overwhelm a prospective client, then you won't get a "yes". Aim to persuade them to agree to just one step first – you can move forward later.

If prospective clients seem to want you to go faster whilst you're explaining your solution, it means they're ready – and eager – for each new pill as you prescribe it. So don't speed up – it means you're going at exactly the right speed.

Step 5: Maximise

Excellent positioning, an insightful diagnosis, and a carefully tailored prescription will often get you straight to a "yes" – but what if it they don't?

To maximise results, the following strategies – used at the end of consultations and in your follow-ups – will convince more prospective clients to say "yes".

Deal with objections before they arise

In my *5 Step Client Conversion Programme*, I teach my clients a strategy for running consultations which does exactly this. But, for the rare occasion when an objection arises after following that process, there's a 7 Step Process for answering objections.

The key point of this process is to plan in advance how to deal with the most likely objections, and not to regard an objection as being the end of the conversation. Instead, treat each objection as the start of a new conversation. A good way to do this is by asking questions such as, *"Could you tell me a little more about that?"*

Help prospective clients take action sooner rather than later

If you want your prospective client to take action now (or soon) then you need to show them why that's important – what's in it for them to act now? You can demonstrate this by, for example, providing examples of what happened to others who waited. Or, if appropriate, you could offer an incentive for them to take action now.

Decide how to follow up if you don't receive an immediate "yes"

To encourage prospective clients to move towards saying "yes", make sure you maintain your positioning as the expert and avoid turning into a salesperson.

To do this, I recommend a range of follow-up strategies using articles, emails, newsletters and invitations to events based around Education-Based Marketing. All of these should continue to educate prospects about why they need your help, why they should accept it sooner rather than later, and why they should choose you.

Action Steps:

1. Refer back to the list of common objections you created in Chapter 4 and plan how you'll respond to them.

2. Decide how you'll encourage your prospective client to take action now – by giving examples of those who waited or an incentive to act now.

3. List at least five methods of following up with prospective clients after their initial consultation. Use this as a menu from which to choose at least three at the end of each consultation.

Success Tip

Timing is critical if you want to maximise your results. This means you need to be ready to deal with objections or delaying tactics on the spot, because it's much more effective to do so there and then rather than trying to do it in your follow-up. However, if a client still insists they want to 'think about it' you should have your follow-up strategy already prepared, so you can put it into action straight away.

Results

When I adopted this 5 Step Client Conversion System in my own business, my success rate at turning enquiries into paying clients went from around 2-in-10 to 8-in-10.

Because I was now spending 20% of my time generating 80% of my work (rather than 80% of it trying to get clients and 20% delivering my services), I also tripled my turnover whilst working the same number of hours.

The value I provided during initial consultations increased dramatically too. Whereas before I'd spent initial meetings answering specific questions – in other words, giving out free advice – I was now helping prospective clients see the *real* issues holding them back from achieving their goals.

Armed with this knowledge, they were far more likely to understand that they needed to make significant changes to their approach to client attraction and conversion in order to get the clients (and profits) they wanted.

This, in turn, meant they were more likely to agree to my help, *and* more likely to achieve their goals. Even if they eventually decided not to work with me, they left the meeting with a deep understanding of the issues they needed to tackle – which was far more valuable than quick-fix tips on, for example, how to improve their use of Google ads or update their website.

The change in my perception of the value of these initial sessions also meant I started to feel much more comfortable in charging for them.

Yes, I still speak to prospective clients without charge – to make sure I can help them before I suggest a paid initial session – but knowing the value I provide means I'm now confident enough to charge for these, and even to offer a money-back guarantee if they're not completely satisfied (which I'm pleased to say has never yet been taken up!).

Once your confidence in the value of what you offer in your consultations is such that you're comfortable to charge for them, you'll find that charging a fee will also help pre-qualify prospective clients and screen out any who aren't serious about taking action. This will help to further increase your conversion rate, and also reduce the time you spend with the wrong kind of prospective clients.

Case Study 1: Increase to virtually 100% conversion rate

After many years working for larger firms – in which most work was brought in by others or by the firm's reputation – Rachael decided to set up her own practice. So now she had to find her own clients. Although she had, very sensibly, been making the most of all her contacts to gain meetings with prospective clients, in these meetings she found she was trying to establish credibility and impress clients by giving away free advice.

In other words, she was 'tap dancing'. And this free advice was pushing away more clients than it was attracting.

Following my 5 Step Client Conversion System gave Rachael a new way to plan, run, and follow up on initial meetings. The results were dramatic. Even whilst still learning the system her conversion rate shot up from *"1-in-too many"* to virtually 100%. In the words of her business partner:

> *"The whole course is extremely valuable. It's been a revelation, as if one had been working in a fog all these years and now*

*it's cleared to reveal crystal-clear scenery. **Every client meeting that we've had since – and even during the course has converted!"***

I'm delighted that Rachael is now charging for her initial consultations – something I recommend to all my clients once they've mastered the 5 Step Client Conversion System.

Case Study 2: Doubling conversion rate to 8/10

When Jay, the managing partner of a law firm, asked me for advice about initial phone consultations, I showed him how to ask the same powerful questions and how to present his solution in the same easily-digestible form that I've just shown you. As a result, his conversion rate doubled. He said afterwards:

> *"With one simple strategy, Michelle's **helped me to transform my client conversion rate on initial enquiry calls from 4/10 to 8/10 – and practically overnight.** She really knows her stuff and I'm very grateful to her."*

There's no reason why *you* can't get similar – or even better – results when you adopt my 5 Step Client Conversion System.

Further help and resources

As with any system, it can take time to master my 5 Step Client Conversion System, and you'll need to commit both time and effort if you want to develop your skills.

When I work with clients to implement these five steps into their initial consultations, we go deeply into each step and I help them plan out exactly what to do (and what not to do) to make it work as effectively as possible for their target market.

If you'd like help in tailoring my system to your specific area of practice, or to the specific type of client you most want to convert, then you can find out more about my *5 Step Client Conversion Programme* here: www. profitablelegalpractice.com/convert

In this 90 day programme I'll show you exactly how to plan, conduct, and follow up initial consultations. You'll also be able to get my personal advice on how to make sure you have a 5 Step Client Conversion System that turns enquiries into paying clients at the highest possible rate.

NEXT

Chapter 8
The Power Of The Client Magnet Formula

You've now learned the five steps of both my Client Attraction and Client Conversion Systems which, together, make up the Client Magnet Formula. As a brief reminder, there are three key phases:

Phase 1: Understand

Always make sure you understand what your ideal clients need to know in order to want your services. It's the foundation upon which the entire formula is built.

After all, if prospective clients don't understand why they need help, or why they should choose you to provide it, then the chances of them deciding to instruct you are negligible.

Phase 2: Attract

Use Education-Based Marketing. Not only will it help you reach more of your ideal clients, it'll also attract clients who, by the time they approach you, will have a good understanding of why they might need your services and be ready to explore whether you're the right person for them.

Create your Education-Based Marketing in the form of a report or guide. In other words, as a tangible object that you can exchange for prospective clients' contact details. Without these, it's so much harder (and slower) to build a relationship.

If you follow these principles you could attract 30%, 50% or even 100% more clients than you're attracting now. All without having to spend significantly more time on marketing, because a Client Magnet can be used in a highly leveraged way.

Phase 3: Convert

It's crucial to follow up your Education-Based Marketing with a 'conversation that converts'. This should serve to deepen prospective clients' understanding of why they need help, the impact of the problems or challenges they face, and the value (to them) of getting your help.

The Power of using all 3 Phases

Once you've learned to implement all three phases effectively, you'll find a much higher proportion of your ideal clients enquire about your services and become paying clients.

A 50% increase in your number of enquiries combined with a 50% increase in conversion rate would *more than double* your number of new clients.

For example:

- If you currently get 40 enquiries a month and convert 50% of them into clients, that gives you 20 clients.

- If you increase your enquiries by 50% you'll now have 60 enquiries.

- If you increase your conversion by 50% you'll have a 75% conversion rate.

- 75% conversion of 60 enquiries will give you 45 new clients, which is more than double your previous results of 20 new clients.

So for maximum effect you must increase *both* your number of enquiries and your conversion rate.

What would increasing both of these mean for your practice?

Chapter 9
A More Profitable Practice

In this book we've learned that getting more clients is the first step towards growing your practice.

But for a truly profitable practice you need to do more than this. You need to maximise profits from existing clients, too.

Getting more clients without also focusing on increasing profits from existing clients will likely lead to one or more of the following:

- you're constantly busy but aren't seeing the profits you'd like

- you work far too many hours for the financial rewards you receive

- you want to hire people so you can delegate some of your work and focus on growth but the business can't afford it

- you're in danger of burning out physically and/or financially.

If your goal is to have more clients *and* more profits, but without working more hours or falling victim to any of the above, then you need to focus on the three elements which I teach in my *Profitable Practice Programme* for lawyers.

The 3 Elements of a Profitable Practice

In order to have a truly profitable practice, you need to have in place the 3 Essential Elements of 'Attract', 'Convert' and 'Maximise'.

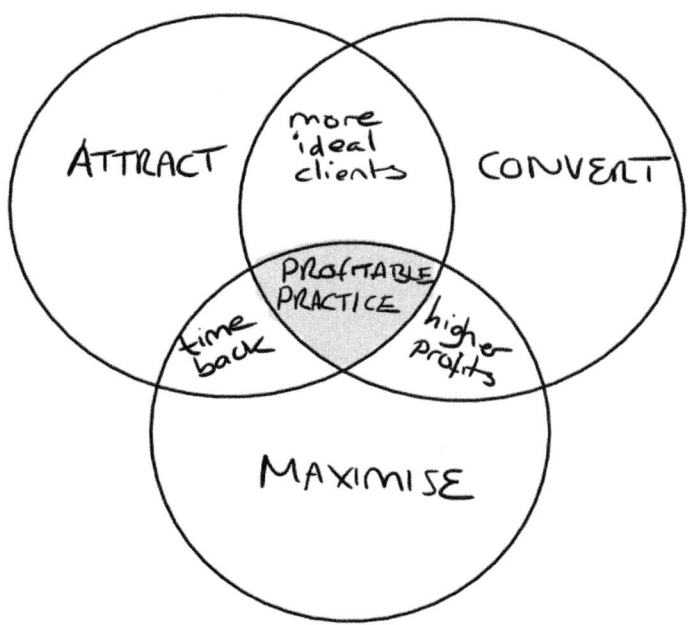

It's only when you combine these three elements that you get the ultimate result that most practice owners strive for: more of your ideal clients, increased profits, and time back (time to do other things outside your practice, or time to work with more clients – it's up to you).

In this book we've discussed the first two, 'Attract' and 'Convert', which are two of the seven Profit Zones you can use to increase the profitability of your practice.

However, the third element, 'Maximise', contains five more Profit Zones based around – as you'd perhaps expect – increasing profits from existing clients. These five Profit Zones are:

1. **Frequency**: encouraging clients to buy your services more frequently (either the same service – if applicable – or a different service)

2. **Size**: offering additional services over and above those they first came to you for, so that they spend more with you

3. **Margin**: increasing profits from each client (whether by raising fees, lowering costs or increasing efficiencies)

4. **Referrals**: getting more referrals from each client

5. **Lifetime**: retaining clients for longer.

Combining the above with 'Attract' and 'Convert' gives us the full 7 Profit Zones:

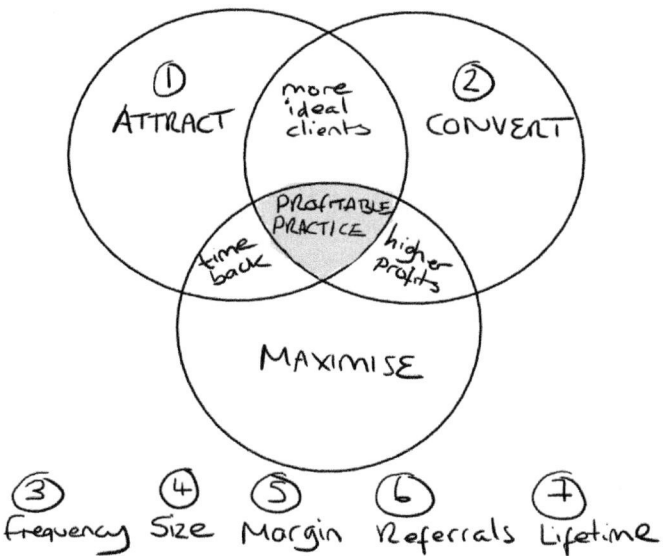

The Leveraging Effect: Why you should work on all 7 Profit Zones

Choosing to grow or improve any one of the Profit Zones will have a positive effect on profitability. But if you really want to see dramatic growth, you need to work on all seven. This is because:

- it's easier and cheaper to get an existing client to buy more of your services than to gain a new client; and

- achieving significant growth through new clients alone requires a lot of time, money and effort (and even then it isn't guaranteed).

For example, imagine you want to double your profits. If you plan to do this by getting new clients, you'll need to double the number of clients you have. Unless you've only just started and have very few clients to begin with, this is a seriously big target. In addition, even if it is achievable, you'll need a large marketing budget and will have to spend a lot of time dealing with all the enquiries you'll need to generate.

But what if you could increase your profits by more than 75% through acquiring only 20% more clients, or could more than double your profits with only 50% more clients? Sounds rather more achievable – and realistic – doesn't it?

My *Profitable Practice Programme* teaches you how to make small improvements to all 7 Profit Zones; improvements which together have a dramatic effect. A 10% increase in each, for example, could grow your profits by more than 75% – and mean most of that growth would come from areas other than getting new clients.

Let me give you an example of how this might work.

Let's assume that:

- you attract 100 enquiries a year for one particular service

- you convert 25 (25%) of these into paying clients, each of whom spends an average of £1,500 with you twice a year at a 30% profit margin

- you receive 50 referrals a year from these clients, of which you again convert 25%.

- overall, these clients generate £112,500 fee income per year of which £33,750 is profit

- these clients stay with you for an average of three years, and continue to instruct you at the same rate, so your clients' lifetime value (profit from them over that time) is £101,250.

This is summarised in the following table:

	New Clients		
Profit Zone	Description		Current
1	Annual Number of Enquiries		100
2	Conversion Ratio		25%
	Number of Clients		25
3	Number of Matters Per Year		2
4	Average Matter Value		£1,500
	Annual Fee Income		£75,000
5	Profit Margin		30%
	Annual Profits		£22,500
6	Annual Number of Referrals		50
	Conversion Ratio of Referrals		25%
	Number of Clients From Referrals		12.5
	Annual Fee Income From Referrals		£37,500
	Annual Profits From Referrals		£11,250
	Total Annual Fee Income/Turnover		£112,500
	Total Annual Profits		£33,750
7	Average Buying Lifetime (Years)		3
	Lifetime Value of Clients (without Referrals)		£67,500
	Total Lifetime Value of Clients (with Referrals)		£101,250

However, implementing some simple and inexpensive strategies in your practice, which increase each Profit Zone by 10%, would increase your fee income to £164,711 (an increase of 46%) and your annual profits to £54,355 (an increase of 61%). And this would come from just 45 clients in total (an increase of 20%). Even better, the profit from these clients over their three year lifetime with you would also increase to £179,371 (an increase of 77%).

You can see a summary of this increase in my Practice Growth Calculator below:

Practice Growth Calculator

Profit Zone	Description	Current	Increase	Results	Cumul. Increase
	New Clients				
1	Annual Number of Enquiries	100	10%	110	
2	Conversion Ratio	25%	2.5%	27.5%	
	Number of Clients	25		30	
3	Number of Matters Per Year	2	10%	2.2	
4	Average Matter Value	£1,500	10%	£1,650	
	Annual Fee Income	£75,000		£109,808	146%
5	Profit Margin	30%	3%	33%	
	Annual Profits	£22,500		£36,236	161%
6	Annual Number of Referrals	50	10%	55	
	Conversion Ratio of Referrals	25%	2.5%	27.5%	
	Number of Clients From Referrals	12.5		15	
	Annual Fee Income From Referrals	£37,500		£54,904	146%
	Annual Profits From Referrals	£11,250		£18,118	161%
	Total Annual Fee Income/Turnover	**£112,500**		**£164,711**	**146%**
	Total Annual Profits	**£33,750**		**£54,355**	**161%**
7	Average Buying Lifetime (Years)	3	10%	3.3	
	Lifetime Value of Clients (without Referrals)	£67,500		£119,580	177%
	Total Lifetime Value of Clients (with Referrals)	£101,250		£179,371	177%

What if you want to double your profits?

As I've already mentioned, doubling your profits by doubling your number of clients is rarely the best way to grow. Not only is the work involved considerable, but the time it takes to attract and convert those clients eats into your fee-earning time and reduces your profits.

Instead, I recommend you take the easier option of doubling your profits with only around 50% more clients.

To illustrate how to achieve this, my Practice Growth Calculator below uses the same figures as before *except* the conversion rate (see Profit Zone 2 which is circled) which I've increased from 25% to 35%. This raises the number of clients to 39 and the number of referred clients to 19 – an overall increase of 52%.

If you now look at the increase in income and profits (highlighted by the black arrow), you'll see the annual profits have more than doubled, while the lifetime value of these clients has increased by 125%. In other words, you've earned more than twice as much profit with only around 50% more clients.

Practice Growth Calculator

Profit Zone	Description	Current	Increase	Results	Cumul. Increase
	New Clients				
1	Annual Number of Enquiries	100	10%	110	
2	Conversion Ratio	25%	10%	35%	
	Number of Clients	25		39	
3	Number of Matters Per Year	2	10%	2.2	
4	Average Matter Value	£1,500	10%	£1,650	
	Annual Fee Income	£75,000		£139,755	186%
5	Profit Margin	30%	3%	33%	
	Annual Profits	£22,500		£46,119	205%
6	Annual Number of Referrals	50	10%	55	
	Conversion Ratio of Referrals	25%	10%	35%	
	Number of Clients From Referrals	12.5		19	
	Annual Fee Income From Referrals	£37,500		£69,878	186%
	Annual Profits From Referrals	£11,250		£23,060	205%
	Total Annual Fee Income/Turnover	£112,500		£209,633	186%
	Total Annual Profit	£33,750		£69,179	205%
7	Average Buying Lifetime (Years)	3	10%	3.3	
	Lifetime Value of Client (without Referrals)	£67,500		£152,193	225%
	Total Lifetime Value of Clients (with Referrals)	£101,250		£228,290	225%

What would your profit be if you added these kinds of increases to your 7 Profit Zones?

Action Steps:
1. Work out your current numbers for each of the 7 Profit Zones. 2. Calculate the additional fee income and profit your practice could generate by increasing each of the 7 Profit Zones by downloading my Practice Growth Calculator here: <u>www. clientmagnetformula.com</u>

Your Practice Growth Gameplan

If you've been inspired by the idea of using all 7 Profit Zones, then I recommend you create a 'Practice Growth Gameplan' – a strategic plan setting out exactly what your practice needs in order to achieve your specific growth goals. For maximum effect, your Gameplan should cover how you plan to increase all seven of the Profit Zones (including how you'll use the 'Attract' and 'Convert' systems I've introduced in this book).

A good Gameplan needs to address the following (in this order):

1. **Goals**: what do you want to achieve in the next 12-36 months in terms of increasing your fee income, profits, quantity or quality of clients, and/ or decreasing your working hours?

2. **Challenges**: what might slow you down, or stop you, from achieving those goals as quickly and easily as you'd like?

3. **Strategies**: taking into account your specific goals and challenges (which are the foundation blocks upon which a strong Gameplan is built),

which strategies will bring you the best results in the shortest time? When I work with clients to help them create their Gameplan I recommend specific 'Accelerators' from my *Profitable Practice Programme* for them to use to increase the speed of their results in each of the Profit Zones. What would accelerate your results?

If you'd like my expert help to create your own Gameplan, there are three ways I can help:

1. Learn how to create your own Gameplan at my online seminar, **The Profitable Practice Gameplan: More Clients, More Profits, More Time**. This runs on various dates throughout the year and you can check dates and register at: www.thebusinessinstructor.com/webinar

2. Attend my one day **Profitable Practice Secrets** workshop. We'll work on creating your Gameplan and installing three of the 9 most important 'Accelerators' to bring you more clients and increased profits. You can check dates and register at: www.thebusinessinstructor.com/secrets

3. Work with me privately, so I can help you create your Gameplan by identifying the 'Accelerators' you need and then help you to *implement* them quickly and effectively through my **Profitable Practice Programme**. This option is ideal if you'd like to double your profits in the next 12 months. To find out more, email me at michelle@thebusinessinstructor.com with *'Private Help'* in the subject line and we'll set up a time to discuss whether this option is a good fit for you.

Take Action

Doubling your profits doesn't need to be a pipe dream. One of my clients – Reena, the Managing Partner of a boutique corporate firm – increased her profits by nearly five times after getting my help. She said:

> *"After my first gameplan session with Michelle, I felt a weight lifted off my shoulders. We mapped out where the business was heading, where I wanted it to go and what I needed to do to get it there. I felt anxious about the size of the goals we'd set, but exuberant and ready to achieve what I thought was the impossible with her guidance. In fact, I decided to join her Profitable Practice Programme so I could get help implementing my Gameplan.*
>
> *With Michelle's patience, steer and motivation to keep aiming higher, I achieved an **increase of 140% in fee income and 471% in profits**. Needless to say I'm planning to work with her for many years to come!"*

If you'd like to achieve these kinds of results too, get in touch using one of the methods above.

But whatever you decide to do next, make sure it involves taking action.

Action changes things.

ACKNOWLEDGMENTS

I'd like to thank my father for bringing out my (previously well-hidden!) entrepreneurial spirit and teaching me so much about marketing, sales, and the importance of generating profit not just revenue.

I'd also like to thank my husband, David, for his unwavering support in everything I do.

And finally thank you to the hundreds of clients who've put their trust in me to help them grow their businesses, and who've been prepared to do the work to make their practice growth goals a reality. You're proof that action changes things.

ABOUT THE AUTHOR

Michelle Peters practised as a solicitor for many years at a large international firm in London. As The Business Instructor, she now helps lawyers to attract more clients and increase their profits without working more hours.

Michelle provides a blend of strategic advice, skills training (including marketing and conversion skills) and mentoring through her *Profitable Practice Programme*. This helps the owners of small law firms – and heads of department in mid-sized firms – to know what to do, how to do it, and (most importantly) gives them the support and accountability to actually get it done.

Michelle developed her business skills outside of the law – only discovering after she had left private practice how little lawyers are taught about the key skills needed to be successful in the business of law: attracting enquiries from ideal clients, converting them into paying clients at the right fees, and maximising profits from each client so that the practice can thrive rather than just survive. Having learned these skills she was inspired to help other lawyers to develop the strategy and skills that would help them be successful at not just the *practise* of law but also the *business* of law.

She is the founder of the Entrepreneurial Lawyers Network (which you can join on LinkedIn) and the author of many reports and guides to help lawyers grow their practice. Find out more at www.thebusinessinstructor.com

Printed in Great Britain
by Amazon

32494566R00078